SECTARIAN GULF

SECTARIAN GULF

*Bahrain, Saudi Arabia, and
the Arab Spring That Wasn't*

TOBY MATTHIESEN

stanford briefs
An Imprint of Stanford University Press
Stanford, California

Stanford University Press
Stanford, California

Printed in the United States of America
on acid-free, archival-quality paper

Library of Congress Cataloging-in-Publication Data
Matthiesen, Toby, 1984– author.
  Sectarian gulf : Bahrain, Saudi Arabia, and the Arab Spring that wasn't /
Toby Matthiesen.
      pages cm
  Includes bibliographical references and index.
  ISBN 978-0-8047-8573-0 (pbk. : alk. paper)
  1. Bahrain—Politics and government—21st century. 2. Saudi Arabia—
Politics and government—21st century. 3. Protest movements—Bahrain.
4. Protest movements—Saudi Arabia. 5. Shi'ah—Relations—Sunnites.
6. Sunnites—Relations—Shi'ah. 7. Arab Spring, 2010- 8. Persian Gulf
States—Politics and government—21st century. I. Title.
  DS247.B28M38 2013
  953.6—dc23   2013016638

  ISBN 978-0-8047-8722-2 (electronic)

Typeset by Classic Typography in 10/13 Adobe Garamond

CONTENTS

DEDICATED TO ADA, CLAUDIA,
KAI, KHADIJA, AND ULF

PREFACE

The mass protests against authoritarian rule that swept the Arab world in 2011 have changed the Middle East, and perhaps the world, forever. They contributed to the biggest global turmoil since the collapse of the Soviet Union, a wave of demonstrations, economic crises, and austerity measures with wide-ranging implications for the future. 2011 was the "year of dreaming dangerously," a year in which various counter-hegemonic ideologies briefly challenged the capitalist world-system.[1] These protests included the Occupy movement, which took some inspiration from the Arab uprisings, as well as mass protests and strikes all over the globe.[2] It seems as if Arabs, and indeed young people across the world, had been waiting for something to rally around, something that could galvanize protests. The Arab uprisings have reaffirmed the importance of people power, the sense that taking to the streets and demanding change can really make a difference, and that the powerful are so only as long as people believe they are untouchable. For decades, public discourse in the Middle East had been cleansed of actual politics, deals were made in secret, crony ministers or royals—and there are many—could not be criticized. The Arab uprisings changed all that, and a new Arab public sphere emerged in which Arab autocrats could no longer feel safe. But

counter-revolutionary forces quickly swept through Middle Eastern streets, trying to divide the protesters along regional, sectarian,
tribal, or ideological lines.

The largest protest movements developed in the Arab republics
Tunisia, Egypt, Libya, and Yemen, where dictators were ousted,
while the Syrian uprising became more and more a civil war. In
contrast, as of 2013, no ruler in an Arab monarchy had to step
down because of the pressure exerted by his own people, even
though a youth movement arose in Morocco and protests in Jordan grew in 2012. In general, then, the monarchies that make up
the Gulf Cooperation Council, the GCC—Saudi Arabia, Bahrain,
Kuwait, Oman, Qatar, and the United Arab Emirates (UAE)—are
more often than not presented as stable, largely unchallenged by
the Arab Spring protests.[3] The truth is, however, that all the GCC
countries have been affected by the Arab Spring and—with the
exception of Qatar and the UAE—saw protest movements
emerge. The regimes in Tunisia, Egypt, and Yemen may have been
key anchors of American hegemony in the region, in the "fight
against terror," and in ensuring Israel's security. But protests in the
Gulf states were even more threatening to American hegemony
than the revolutions in Tunisia and Egypt because the states bordering the Gulf[4] contain about two-thirds of the world's proven
oil reserves and a third of the proven natural gas reserves. They are
also home to major U.S. army bases, key buyers of Western arms
and increasingly important trading partners with significant
investments in Western economies.[5]

Bahrain almost experienced a revolution in early 2011. And
even those countries that did not see protest movements emerge
were transformed by security responses in anticipation of protest
movements, such as in the UAE. But Western political elites, and
both the Western and pan-Arab media, are for strategic reasons
often reluctant to discuss the protests and demands for political
reform in the Gulf. As David Cameron paradigmatically defined
the position of Western policymakers in April 2012, "Bahrain is
not Syria."[6]

This book tells the story of how the Arab Spring affected these Gulf countries, above all Bahrain, Saudi Arabia, Kuwait, and Oman, and how Gulf regimes responded both at home and in the wider Middle East to calls for political change. It is not a comprehensive history of the Arab Spring, or of everything that has happened in the Gulf states since the start of the Arab Spring. Rather, it uses some of the examples of popular protest in the Gulf to show that the legitimacy of Gulf rulers has been challenged profoundly.

Reacting to these historical challenges and demands for democracy, a fairer distribution of resources, and the rule of law, Gulf ruling families and the regimes around them resorted to old tactics of denial, repression, economic largesse, and defamation. None of the Gulf states initiated significant domestic political reforms or managed to engage the emerging youth movements in a manner that would pave the way for a stable future. While the Gulf regimes often embraced the new politics and discourse of the Arab Spring abroad, they refused to acknowledge that this new era in Arab history also had a profound impact at home.

In response to the Arab Spring protests, the Gulf ruling families, above all the Bahraini and Saudi ruling families, have played on and strengthened sectarian divisions between Sunni and Shia to prevent a cross-sectarian opposition front, something that seemed possible in the first days of the uprising in Bahrain, thereby creating a *sectarian Gulf*. But while sectarianism in the Gulf owes much to regime-sponsored or approved sectarian rhetoric, and a political campaign indiscriminately targeting the Gulf Shia, other factors are at play as well.

The sectarian Gulf was encouraged by sectarian identity entrepreneurs,[7] namely people who used sectarian identity politics to bolster their own positions. A close look at their role indicates that sectarianism was not just a government invention but the result of an amalgam of political, religious, social, and economic elites who all used sectarianism to further their personal aims.

Because the media are controlled, the sectarianism in Gulf media since 2011 can only be attributed to decisions of political elites. But once sectarianism has become a viable way of tarnishing the image of political adversaries, it moves to all levels of society and becomes as much a bottom-up as a top-down process.

My interest in the new sectarianism sweeping through the Middle East stems from my studies and travels in that region. After 9/11, key debates focused on "Islam" as a "threat" to the West, the so-called Clash of Civilizations, and whether Islam was a refutation of secularization theories and the idea that Western-style liberal democracy and capitalism would prevail unchallenged—amounting, all in all, to an "end of history" as we knew it.[8] Discussions of Sunni-Shia conflicts were in many cases still confined to academia, or to individual countries such as Lebanon, Iraq, or Pakistan. At the time, I was not particularly interested in the differences between Sunni and Shia, but more in the problematic image of the Middle East and Islam in the West, and in the two wars in Iraq and Afghanistan that were being waged in response to 9/11. While the 9/11 attacks were carried out by an organization that was virulently anti-Shia—al-Qaeda—they were mainly directed against the West. It was only the civil war between Shia and Sunni in Iraq after the fall of Saddam Hussein that really made sectarianism one of *the* key features of Middle East politics.[9] And the response of the Gulf states to the Arab Spring has reinforced this situation, arguably making sectarianism in the region more important than ever before.

In February 2006 I was studying at the University of Isfahan in Iran for a few weeks to improve my Persian and to get to know this important yet often misunderstood country. Much of the splendor of Isfahan's palaces and gardens stem from the sixteenth century, when Isfahan became the capital of the Safavid dynasty. Sunni and Shia split very early in the formation of Islam over the leadership of the community of Muslims after the Prophet Muhammad. The Shia do not recognize the first three caliphs, Abu Bakr, Umar, and Uthman, as successors of the Prophet Muhammad but rather see

Ali, whom the Sunnis see as the fourth caliph, as the righteous successor after the death of Prophet Muhammad. Under Ali's reign, the party of Ali, Shiat Ali, split away from the majority of Muslims, who would become known as the Sunnis. Throughout Islamic history, the Shia remained the minority amongst Muslims and often lived at the periphery of empires and in opposition to the powers of the day. But they developed a distinct school of jurisprudence, a powerful clergy, and their own religious rituals and festivities.[10] It was the Safavids that converted much of the Iranian population to Shia Islam and made Shiism the state religion in Iran. They did this in part by staffing the new religious bureaucracy with Shia clerics from the old centers of Shia scholarship in Lebanon, Iraq, and Bahrain, where Shiism had survived over the centuries.[11]

During my studies in Iran, I had the feeling that the self-understanding of the Islamic Republic of Iran and its political problems stemmed from a number of factors: negotiating religion and politics, resisting the secular legacy of the Shah and replacing it with solidarity with the Global South and a nationalism inspired by Islam, a disdain for Israel and America, and tensions between the people and a repressive regime. All of this was in 2009 to erupt into open conflict when the Green Movement attempted to change the system through large street protests.[12] But it did not really occur to me that the state legitimized itself vis-à-vis the Sunnis. Iran has its own sizable minorities of Kurds, Azeris, and Baluchs, as well as Shia and Sunni Arabs near the Gulf coast. These communities face discrimination of their own.[13] The largely Sunni Arabs in the southern Khuzestan province were also inspired by the Arab Spring and protested in April 2011 to commemorate the memory of an earlier uprising there in 2005. They were repressed harshly.[14] Sunnis from the Gulf often ask why the Gulf states should treat their Shia citizens better while Iran suppresses its Sunnis.[15] Shia Islam is key to how state and society function in Iran. But again, I did not get a sense that the main

"others" were the Sunnis per se. A disdain for and ritualized bash-
ing of America and Israel seemed much more important.

However, one morning in late February 2006, as I left the
guesthouse for foreign students and walked over to the language
center, things had changed visibly. The day before, Sunni militants
affiliated with al-Qaeda had entered the al-Askari shrine in the
Iraqi city of Samarra and set off explosives, causing the massive
golden dome above the shrine to collapse.[16] The shrine is one of
Shia Islam's holiest sites, as it is the burial place for the tenth and
eleventh imams that are revered by Twelver Shia Muslims. Twelver
Shia are the mainstream of Shia Islam and honor twelve imams as
successors of the Prophet Muhammad and leaders of the Muslim
community after the Prophet's death.

The attacks caused outrage across the Muslim world, but particularly amongst Shia Muslims, and led to a renewed campaign
of sectarian violence in Iraq, including reprisal attacks by Shia on
Sunnis.[17] The day after the attack, I saw along my route to Persian
lessons that pictures showing the crumbled dome of the shrine,
which every Shia Muslim knows, had been put up across Isfahan
University and indeed the town itself. Iranian media were outraged, and people were shocked by this deliberate attack on a holy
site. In the weeks that followed, I had many discussions in which
Iranians started to denounce al-Qaeda and its alleged Sunni backers in the Gulf.

Over the following years, I traveled to the other side of the
Gulf, to Saudi Arabia, Bahrain, and Kuwait, societies characterized by centuries of trade, travel, and migration that were hetero-
geneous and escaped easy categorizations. And yet, in the
discourse of their politicians and in the media, Saudi Arabia and
Iran had become reduced to "Sunni" and "Shia" countries that
were vying for influence amongst their respective sects in the
wider region. Although Saudi Arabia and Iran use religion to further their aims, the reality is more nuanced.

What distinguishes the new sectarianism from previous periods
of sectarian tensions is that rulers now make decisions on the basis

of a sectarian assessment of politics. They think strategically in sectarian terms, and shape their foreign policies in those terms. As a result, majority Shia Iran is viewed as an infidel arch-rival, although paradoxically followed closely by the Sunni Islamist Muslim Brotherhood, which since its election victories in Egypt and Tunisia has become the other enemy of choice for Gulf elites, who attribute much of the same malicious transnational meddling to the Muslim Brotherhood that they also ascribe to Iran. That the discourse surrounding the alleged meddling of Iran and the Muslim Brotherhood is so similar, even though the interests and allies of the two players are so radically different, nurtures the suspicion that these allegations are often about finding a scapegoat to deflect popular attention to an external enemy.[18]

As a consequence of the new sectarianism, sectarian violence is increasing across the region, and the social fabric between Sunni and Shia has broken down in many Middle Eastern states. While the West has not directly taken up the sectarian rhetoric, it has accepted the sectarian logic of marginalizing the Shia and by default Iran. This is part of a larger scheme to isolate Iran, including by fighting a proxy conflict in Syria, and the United States and the EU therefore do not heavily pressure their allies in the Gulf to tame sectarianism.

Of course, sectarianism has for centuries been a driving force of civil war and violence in Europe, the Middle East, and the Indian subcontinent. In many ways a reference to sectarianism is often meant to imply that the conflicts between religions and within religions are based on ancient hatred, on an irrationality that escapes analysis, and that the study of sectarian conflicts is futile, since such conflicts are based on cultural essentials.

But the kind of political sectarianism this book talks about only arises under certain conditions, particularly when it is coupled with political economy, with the notion of who gets what, when, where, and from whom. Political sectarianism in the Levante, for example, was strengthened under Ottoman and French colonial rule because of the institutionalization of sects in the political and judicial systems and through the disenfranchisement of some sects and the domination by others.[19] Lebanon has for decades served as a reminder that political sectarianism and civil war are fueled by the involvement of external actors, including former European colonial powers, the United States, Israel, Iran, Syria, and Saudi Arabia.[20]

In the Gulf, the British institutionalized and ensured the survival of pro-British Sunni monarchies that became dependencies of the British Empire in the late eighteenth and early nineteenth centuries. These Gulf monarchies were always dependent on external support to defend themselves against larger neighbors and against internal uprisings. When Britain withdrew its armed forces from the Gulf in 1971 and Bahrain, Qatar, the UAE, and Oman became independent from Britain, the Americans took over as the Gulf's security guarantor. Henceforth, the three regional powers, Iran, Iraq, and Saudi Arabia, competed even more openly for power.[21]

A history of proxy conflicts with Iran after 1979 and a deep fear of Iranian hegemonic ambitions in the Gulf lead to a paranoia in the mind-sets of Gulf rulers when it comes to Iran.[22] At the same time, Gulf rulers harbor an equally strong suspicion of street politics à la Tahrir square that give people agency and voice, and that is fundamentally at odds with the absolutist monarchical systems they are part of. This explains why Gulf rulers were so afraid when a mass protest movement with the strong participation of Gulf Shia combined their fears of the Shia and Iran with a disdain for street politics, and why they reacted to the Arab Spring with repression and sectarianism that divided their societies into Sunni and Shia "camps," literally creating a sectarian Gulf.

SECTARIAN GULF

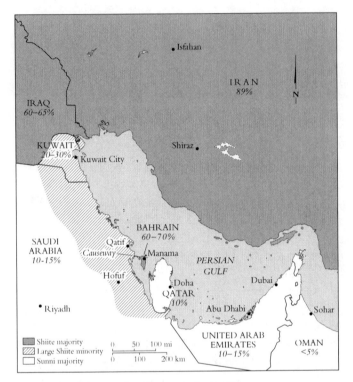

Percentages of Shia Muslim Citizens in the Gulf States

1　OIL, GOD, AND PEARLS

The first time I flew to Manama, the capital of the small island state of Bahrain, was in 2008, en route to do fieldwork on the Shia in the Gulf, specifically those in the Eastern Province of Saudi Arabia, which is linked to Bahrain via a causeway. I sat next to a sixty-year-old American from the Midwest, who was heading to the oil fields in Dhahran in the Eastern Province. I had never seen anyone drink so much on a plane—he gave me the impression that this was the last bar before hell and we had better make the most of it. He would be taking a service taxi from the Manama airport across the causeway and into the Kingdom of Saudi Arabia, where alcohol consumption is a severe offense. As I was to fly from Bahrain to Riyadh just three days later and then stay there for several months, I thought it was wise to join him, the other expats, and the few Arab professionals in the surrounding rows in knocking back the complimentary whisky and gin while the lights of the oil refineries lining the Gulf flickered below. He had done

1

this trip dozens of times and knew all the oil fields and refineries, from the south of Iraq and Abadan on Iran's Gulf shore to Kuwait, and down the coast to the Eastern Province of Saudi Arabia and Bahrain. There is perhaps no better way to understand the density of the oil fields and the importance of the region to the global oil industry than on a night flight, when the fires of the refineries light up the sky.

Shia Muslims are strongly represented in the stretch of land that we were flying over, though they make up only a minority of Muslims all over the world—somewhere between 10 to 13 percent of the roughly 1.6 billion Muslims.[1] Shia are the majority in southern Iraq, particularly around Basra, where a large part of Iraq's oil is located and where Saddam Hussein brutally cracked down on a largely Shia uprising in 1991 after the first Gulf War. The Americans watched that crackdown from the sidelines, but when they invaded Iraq in 2003 the Shia of Iraq were brought to power, and the Gulf Shia were able to reestablish old ties with their Iraqi counterparts, through pilgrimage, religious education, business, and intermarriage, and were inspired by the political empowerment of Iraqi Shia. If the Saudi ruling family saw the deposing of Saddam as a historical mistake and an attack on the predominance of the Sunnis in the Middle East, then the Saudi Shia minority in the Eastern Province welcomed the invasion, telling the American diplomats in the country how relieved they were to see Iraqi Shia able to live their religion freely and choose their own political destiny, and that they hoped to achieve the same in Saudi Arabia, too.[2]

Along the Gulf coast of Saudi Arabia, stretching from Kuwait down to Bahrain, Qatar, and the UAE, up to half of the citizen population is Shia. In Kuwait, the Shia are between 20 and 30 percent of the population. They have long been allied with the ruling family, so many have become wealthy. In Bahrain, Shia make up between 60 and 70 percent of the citizen population, and their case is politically much more sensitive. They would have the potential to overturn the political system both by street protests

Percentage of Shia in the Gulf

Country	Percentage of Citizens Who Are Shia
Iran	89
Bahrain	60–70
Iraq	60–65
Kuwait	20–30
Saudi Arabia	10–15
UAE	10–15
Qatar	10
Oman	< 5

NOTE: No official statistics distinguish between Sunni and Shia when estimating the number of Muslims in the Gulf countries. These are estimates for the Shia population in the states with access to the Gulf, based on the available literature and fieldwork across the Gulf.

and democratic means if they were to act as a cohesive group and were allowed adequate representation in a democratic system.[3] In Saudi Arabia there are between two and three million Shia, the majority of whom live in the Eastern Province, centered around the two oases al-Ahsa and Qatif.[4]

It was next to these Shia settlements in the Eastern Province in the 1950s that the Americans and their Saudi royal partners established new oil towns—Dhahran, Khobar, and Dammam—as well as a huge compound for the Arabian American Oil Company (ARAMCO), the formerly American and now Saudi-owned oil company. This is where my seatmate on my flight to Manama was headed. As he explained to me, laws were different in those early days, and Westerners could do as they pleased. It was, according to him, the only way one could live in Arabia, in a compound, detached and protected from the Arabs and the desert surrounding them. Compounds and gated communities for American expatriates were introduced to Saudi Arabia by ARAMCO in the 1930s.[5] Most Westerners in the Gulf still live in such gated communities, with high walls and armed guards, deeply ignorant and suspicious of what and who is beyond the walls and windows of their homes and offices. Wine made in bathtubs and pool parties with DJs abound.[6] And I was about to find this out firsthand, living in a compound in Riyadh.

But first, my seatmate recommended a hotel in Bahrain for me, where he said he had gone for the past few years, one that was reasonably priced, with decent food and a friendly staff. We parted ways in the arrival hall in Manama, where travelers were separated into three groups: one for *Khalijis*, Gulf citizens whose name derived from the Arabic name for the Gulf, *al-Khalij*, with passports from the GCC states; one for foreigners, meaning Western expats and visitors; and one for the mainly Indian and South-Asian laborers that arrived with only a handful of belongings to work for a few hundred dollars a month in the burning heat of Arabia as construction workers on the palaces, skyscrapers, and highways or as cleaners, waiters, housemaids, or even soldiers who were relied upon to crush the occasional revolt.[7] In 2008, the slogan of Bahrain was still "Business-friendly Bahrain," and citizens of Western countries were given visas upon arrival, a practice that was made much more difficult after too many journalists, NGOs, and researchers came to investigate the brutal crackdown on protesters in 2011. Perhaps it is needless to say that the slogan was also scrapped after the 2011 uprising, being about as far removed from reality as the slogan that was used to promote the Formula 1 race in 2012: *UniF1ed: One Nation in Celebration.*

I took a cab to the recommended hotel. As I got into the taxi, I wondered what the discussion with the driver would bring, and if, like many modern travelers, I would see his opinions as representative of the current state of the country, if they would confirm what I had read previously about the region. From the ring the cab driver wore on his right hand, I knew that he was Shia. The ring, which can be made of various gemstones and has references to the oneness of God engraved, was a tradition first established by the Shia imams. When I asked him about this, he looked puzzled. His typical foreign customers—Western businessmen, oil workers, and soldiers—generally were not interested in local religious and political affairs. He replied with a lowered voice, "Yes I am a Shia, we are the majority in this country, but the ruling family is Sunni. Therefore, we have many problems with them." I would learn much more about the history and politics of the Gulf Shia over the next years, but even this first conversation made me wonder whether the political marginalization of the Gulf Shia was not a ticking time bomb.

The hotel turned out to be an over-priced high-rise tower in Juffair. I took a room and went down to one of the bars with lower noise levels. Sitting next to me was a German couple. The man was working at the Formula 1 racetrack and she in a local advertising company. He previously had worked at the Hockenheimring racetrack in Germany, but as Formula 1 under Bernie Ecclestone recast itself as a global brand, teaming up with new cash-rich venues such as Bahrain, Abu Dhabi, Singapore, or Shanghai, venues with almost unlimited budgets to bid for F1 races, the man came to seek his own fortune in the Gulf. Bahrain was keen to promote its image as a liberal business center through the F1, a plan that somewhat worked until 2011, when the race was cancelled amidst the mass protests and the following violent crackdown that occurred that year. In 2012 and 2013, the ruling family decided to stage the race again, but the 2012 event became a PR disaster, with foreign media highlighting police brutality and the lack of reform in the desert island.[8]

After a while, the couple left and I returned to my room to sleep. But the reverberating bass line from the music in the hotel nightclub shook the walls of my über-kitsch room, thwarting any attempt at sleep, and so I returned downstairs. The large nightclub looked rather sleazy, with large mirrors on the walls. Two hundred mainly African American soldiers were dancing to Dirty South rap that a soldier doubling as DJ was playing from his booth high up over the crowd. There were also some female soldiers with slightly intimidating looks, and a few dozen Asian girls who tried to attract the soldiers' attention and increasingly my own. I ordered some whisky, and soon found myself talking to some of the soldiers, who recounted stories about the wars in Iraq and Afghanistan and the dullness of life at the American naval base in Bahrain, home to the headquarters of the U.S. Navy's Fifth Fleet. The Fifth Fleet is a key cornerstone for the American army, and is responsible for naval forces in the Gulf, the Red Sea, the Arabian Sea, and the coast off East Africa. Though only a few hours had passed since I had arrived in Bahrain, I had quickly found myself in the middle of the confusing set of strategic interests, resources, wars, and identities that make up the contemporary Middle East. Bahrain and Saudi Arabia's Eastern Province were at the heart of all of this, not least the American hegemonic presence in the region, of which the soldiers with whom I bought rounds of drinks were a most visible sign.

Three years later, on February 15, 2011, when I made another flight to Manama, the world was quite different. Arabs were toppling dictators across the region. Only a few days earlier, Tunisia's Ben Ali had fled to Saudi Arabia, where he remains in exile and is a vital symbol of how contradictory the Saudi approach to the Arab Spring has been. While 2011 saw protest movements from Chile to the United States, Europe, and Russia, the Arabs were really showing the world how to mobilize and how to bring down dictators, and the Egyptians had just ousted Mubarak from power. Even still, politicians and analysts were busy consoling themselves that Country X was not like Country Y, that Tunisia and Egypt were exceptions in the sea of authoritarian states, that Syria and particularly Gulf countries such as Bahrain or Saudi Arabia could not experience protest movements.[9]

A day before I boarded the plane to return to Bahrain, on February 14, 2011, one protester had been killed while trying to march to the Pearl Roundabout, a central traffic intersection in Manama. A bit frightened, I asked the two Bahraini women sitting next to me on the plane what they thought, but they replied that I should not be worried as there are protests all the time, and had been in

Bahrain for decades. They were referring to the period of sustained popular mobilization from 1994 onwards that did not stop until 2000–2001, when the new King Hamad reached out to the opposition groups, brought them back from exile, and promised profound political reforms, which were supposed to follow a National Action Charter. Incidentally, this charter was approved almost unanimously by a referendum on February 14, 2001. But the promises of fundamental political reform were broken, as Hamad Al Khalifa promulgated a new constitution that significantly differed from the charter Bahrainis had voted for, ensuring that the ruling family maintained a tight grip on power and that the elected half of the parliament had only limited powers. Also in 2002, Hamad Al Khalifa changed the name of the country he was ruling from "State of Bahrain" to "Kingdom of Bahrain," and declared himself king rather than amir.[10] The Bahraini regime had intended to use the ten-year anniversary of this referendum as a propaganda tool with planned festivities and advertisements praising the ten-year reform path posted throughout the country, but this idea backfired.

At Manama airport, all seemed normal, and driving to the hotel was no problem. But when I went to the Arab restaurant on the rooftop of my hotel late that night to grab a bite, I could hear sirens and the sound of helicopters circling over the city, and particularly near the Pearl Roundabout.

I had arranged this research trip weeks before, unaware of a Facebook page that called for a Day of Rage on February 14, 2011. I had wanted to interview veterans of the leftist, Arab Nationalist, and communist movements in the Gulf. But when I met a friend of mine for a late lunch on February 16, he understandably did not want to speak about the history of popular protest and leftist political mobilization in Bahrain. Rather, he wanted to discuss current events. And he wanted to go to the Pearl Roundabout, which was now apparently controlled by the protesters and increasingly being referred to as Tahrir Square, in homage to Cairo's epicenter of

People rush toward the Pearl monument in Manama, Bahrain, on February 16, 2011. European Pressphoto Agency/Mazen Mahdi.

protests. Protesters had gathered at the Pearl Roundabout in the afternoon of February 15, after a second protester had been killed, and his funeral procession on the morning of February 16 was attended by over a thousand people who walked from the main hospital and morgue in Bahrain, the Salmaniya Medical Complex, to a cemetery.[11]

My friend and his wife took me in their car that evening, and we drove to the roundabout, leaving the old city of Manama to our left and passing the skyscrapers of the financial district. But a few hundred meters from the roundabout in the financial heart of the city we had to stop; the roads were blocked, not by riot police but by a sheer endless mass of empty cars. Thousands had come out to witness what was going on. Unlike in Cairo, where most protesters came by public transport, here most came by car, and this added a whole new disruptive dimension to the protests. When I pointed out to my friend that the mass of silent cars felt like the start of a "car revolution," he replied with a smile, "This is the Gulf, after all." We got out of the car and started walking toward the white glowing monument at the center of the round-about. Illuminated in the night the white pearl monument had an almost magical appeal. In its center stood a sculpture of a dhow—a traditional local sailing vessel—with six arches for its sails, representing the six members of the Gulf Cooperation Coun-cil. At the top perched a simulated pearl, as pearl diving had been one of the cornerstones of Bahrain's economy before the discovery of oil. Approaching the monument we could hear the voices of thousands, the shrieking of megaphones, fanfares, music, engines. What struck me most when we were finally standing on the Pearl Roundabout was how relaxed everyone seemed to be. There were thousands of people on the roundabout, and two had been killed trying to reach here, but on that evening of February 16 it felt like the most natural thing to bring your family to a demonstration in the heart of the capital. Within a few hours, protesters had already set up tents, screens, makeshift kitchens, medical centers, mobile phone charging stations, and a podium for speakers.

We first went to see my friend's colleagues, a few dozen elderly men in a large tent where all the different leftist opposition groups were gathering. For decades they had been trying to "liberate" Bahrain. Britain had been the colonial power in the Gulf since the late eighteenth century, and it entered into a treaty relationship with the Al Khalifa in 1820, which recognized the Al Khalifa as rulers of Bahrain. Britain also established a Royal Navy base in the country, the premises of which were taken over as the base for the U.S. Navy's Fifth Fleet at formal independence in 1971. So while the leftists had long fought an anti-colonial struggle, they were left in the grip of the Al Khalifa ruling family, who like the other Gulf ruling families were very much a product of British protection.[12] The Gulf was a key arena of the Cold War, as both the Soviet bloc and the "West" wanted to ensure control of its vast oil resources. Leftist groups, from Arab Nationalists, Nasserists, Baathists, to Communists, were very popular in the Gulf from the 1950s to the 1970s and constituted a genuine threat to the survival of pro-Western monarchies. They had been particularly strong in Bahrain, Kuwait, the Eastern Province of Saudi Arabia, the UAE, and Oman. Many Shia had been recruited into these movements that promised equality with their Sunni comrades. Many of the Bahraini veterans had also fought in the Dhufar Rebellion in Oman from 1965 to 1976. From there they wanted to liberate the Arabian Peninsula and the Gulf countries, and finally the rest of the Arab world and Palestine. But British colonial officers and their allies in the Gulf ruling families cracked down hard on the leftists, and the leftists in the Gulf eventually lost their popularity.[13]

This protest at the Pearl Roundabout was the closest to a proper revolution at home they had ever gotten after decades of opposition politics, and they were politicians enough not to let that opportunity go unused. One of the leftist groups—the Arab Nationalist Wa'ad[14]—was, along with the Shia Islamist alliance al-Wifaq,[15] the only political society that had openly supported the February 14 protests. They would pay a heavy price for this in the months that followed, but on that night spirits were running high. In the tent, there were some veteran political activists such as Ibrahim Sharif, the secretary general of Wa'ad and a Sunni from a family originally from Iran. In front of the tent a group of leftist *shabab*, young men, were gathering and had set up loudspeakers from which they were now filling the air with anthems of the revolutionary Arab leftist movements: National liberation, justice, freedom, socialism. They said they had been amongst the first to arrive on the roundabout but conceded that they were just a small group, and that the majority on the roundabout was slowly being mobilized by the Islamist groups. While many of them were Shia, I spoke to several Sunnis, both old and young, who were on the roundabout and supported the key demands of the protesters such as more power for the elected assembly and a new constitution.

Amongst the rather small group of young leftists was a Sunni woman, who reiterated the calls for democracy, human rights, and dignity. Her appearance was a stark contrast to the ways in which the protesters were later portrayed by the regime's media as Iranian-controlled, armed, Islamist, and purely Shia gangs. Three months later I would meet her again, and she would tell me why she fell out with the people on the roundabout and joined the pro-regime protests.

I left the leftists and strolled around. Hundreds of tents and mattresses had been put up in the first two days, and the protesters were determined to camp out for many more. Within a day, makeshift kitchens with huge pots had been set up, handing out cookies, rice with shrimp from the waters around Bahrain, fruit, tea, juice, and water. I was curious how this infrastructure could have been put in place so quickly, and was told by a volunteer that much of this came from the Shia mourning houses, the *ma'tams* or *hussainiyyas*, in the old town of Manama. There in the old lanes of the capital, the Shia commemorate the martyrdom of Imam Hussayn during Muharram and Ashura. Key to these public processions are the mourning houses, where throughout the year religious gatherings take place, and so their staff and volunteers are used to catering for large crowds. They had now moved their equipment to the roundabout, and through this infrastructure made the protest camp possible.

All this leads to the important question: Was this a "Shia" protest right from the start, or was a gloss of sectarianism imposed later on by the state as part of its crackdown? The majority of protesters were Shia—but the majority of citizens in Bahrain are Shia. The demographic mix should not come as a surprise. More important are the demands of the protesters that, at least in the early days, were not sectarian. On that first day, the demand that I heard most frequently was moderate: "The people want the reform of the regime," taking the slogan that had galvanized protesters in Cairo and Tunis ("The people want the fall of the regime") but substituting *islah* (reform) for *isqat* (fall). Protesters demanded the release of political prisoners, a lifting of travel bans, a new constitution, and respect for human rights. There were quite a lot of chants already calling for the resignation of Prime Minister Prince Khalifa bin Salman Al Khalifa, who had been in power for four decades, ever since Bahrain gained its formal independence, making him the longest serving unelected prime minister in the world. Indeed, his resignation became the key rallying cry in the days to come, and pictures and slogans denouncing him were omnipresent on the roundabout.

At the start, reform-minded Sunnis could accept most of the demands of the Pearl Roundabout protesters. And it was this early potential for cross-sectarian mobilization around basic values and demands that seemed most dangerous to the ruling family and indeed the other Gulf monarchies. Bahrain has a history of Sunni-Shia opposition cooperation, particularly in the era of the leftist movements from the 1950s to the 1970s and, on a more limited scale, in the 2000s.[16] The uprising in the 1990s also saw some cooperation between leftists and Shia Islamists. That uprising had many of the same demands as today's protests, and was also partially a fight by the Shia majority to achieve more political rights and counter repression by the regime.[17] As the protest in 2011 progressed, some of the imagery became related to the history of Shia political mobilization in Bahrain: there were posters of those martyred so far and of a number of political prisoners. Other posters depicted martyrs of the 1990s uprising. Women sitting on the grass surrounding the roundabout held up pictures of prisoners who had been arrested in previous months and years. Many of those prisoners would be released a few days later, only to be arrested again in the crackdown that followed in mid-March.

From the beginning a large proportion of the protesters hailed from Islamist backgrounds. Many of the protesters were supporters of al-Wifaq, the Shia Islamist bloc that had tried to work within the current political system. Indeed, al-Wifaq held eighteen out of forty elected seats in the Bahraini parliament, but all al-Wifaq MPs resigned on February 15 after the first protester was shot dead.

On my first night on the roundabout, February 16, the secretary-general of al-Wifaq, Ali Salman, made his first appearance there and spoke to the protesters. He had just come from a meeting with Crown Prince Salman bin Hamad Al Khalifa, where both sides had hoped to find a political solution, joint efforts that would continue intermittently over the next month.[18] But not just members of al-Wifaq were present; there were also others whose aim was to reject the monarchy altogether. Many people at the roundabout were supporters of two banned Islamist parties, Haqq and al-Wafa, who refused engagement with the state and did not participate in elections.[19] Hasan Mushayma, the leader of Haqq, was still in London receiving medical treatment at the start of the protests, and on the roundabout people were waiting for his return. He returned to Bahrain a few weeks into the uprising.

Slogans painted on some of the tents and posters hung from the palm trees surrounding the Pearl Roundabout indicated that

Shaking throne in front of the Pearl monument on February 22, 2011.
Photo by the author.

another Shia group was also active on the roundabout, the so-
called *shirazis*, a transnational Shia movement founded in the
1970s that derives its name from the spiritual leadership of
Muhammad Mahdi al-Shirazi.[20] In 1981, the *shirazis* had planned
a coup to take over power in Bahrain, but the plot was foiled and

many of its members were arrested. Though the *shirazis* always represented a minority in the Bahraini Shia political scene,[21] they were the strongest political force amongst the Shia in the Eastern Province of Saudi Arabia. Seeing *shirazi* slogans in the Pearl Roundabout, it was not much of an intellectual leap to wonder if some parts of the *shirazi* network might soon start protests in the Eastern Province. And indeed, one day later, on February 17, a few dozen youths held a silent demonstration in Awwamiyya, a village that is a hotbed of the more confrontational line of the Saudi *shirazis*.

Apart from the prominence of Shia Islamists, I vividly remember a few dozen young men at the Pearl Roundabout, sitting in front of a projector. There were quite a few TV sets and projectors around the roundabout, and people were often watching one of the international news reports about the events in Bahrain, mainly on Iranian-sponsored news channels such as the Arabic-language al-Alam, since they were almost the only ones covering the events at this point. But this particular group of young men was watching a football match, Arsenal versus Barcelona. Having lived in northeast London for the past few years, I had become a supporter of Arsenal, even if not a particularly fanatical one, and was intrigued to see the passion young Bahrainis had for this match, even in the midst of this political struggle. Football seemed a welcome break from politics, and the crowd was enthusiastically supporting Barcelona, who were outmaneuvering Arsenal.

I left the Pearl Roundabout late in the evening, and went to a hotel bar with a few friends. Thrilled by the joyful atmosphere on the roundabout, I was energized and full of hope for the coming days. At the time it seemed like a crackdown was impossible—surely no one would commit a massacre with old women and young children sleeping on the roundabout. In the hotel bar, the soccer game was on in the background with only thirty minutes to go and Arsenal still losing. I continued to talk politics with the Bahrainis. They were optimistic but said that the ruling family was strong and should not be underestimated; it would not fall like Mubarak in a matter of weeks. Suddenly, I heard a few British expats shouting in the corner of the pub, as Arsenal scored twice and won the game. The win added to my joy, even though the older Bahrainis I was sitting with were not so interested in football, more in how they could finally transform their country.

I returned to my hotel around two in the morning, February 17, to jot down notes about what I had seen, the unexpected scale of protests. Just as I was about to go to sleep around three in the morning a friend called me to say, "A massacre is happening! They are attacking the roundabout." I turned on the television and opened my laptop but no one was reporting the news, and then slowly the first reports emerged on social media. The next few hours I stayed glued to the Internet, and after a while, some English-language stations were beginning to bring news feeds about the crackdown. Al-Jazeera Arabic, though they had placed a twenty-four-hour feed on Cairo's Tahrir Square, was not reporting this story, as the Qataris were nervous about protests spreading in the Gulf states.[22]

Four battalions—the police, the National Security Agency, the Ministry of Interior Criminal Investigations Department, and the Bahrain Defence Force Intelligence—had surrounded the whole area of the Pearl Roundabout, with more Bahrain Defence Force units waiting in the vicinity. A few minutes after urging people to leave the roundabout they moved in from all sides and attacked the protesters with tear gas and rubber bullets, killing three and injuring dozens. They razed the tent city to the ground, burning what was left behind.[23] The Gulf Spring was over before it really started, and the Gulf monarchies had proven that they would shoot their own citizens if they were too vocal in demanding reform. But much worse was yet to come.

Within the space of a day, I had arrived in Bahrain to witness the beginnings of a revolution, political discussions about the future of this country, and protests at the Pearl Roundabout, and then seen the brutal start of the counter-revolution that would soon engulf other countries in the region. It was hard to sleep that night in downtown Manama, as the Western-made helicopters buzzed over my hotel and the Twitter-feed filled with horrific news and grim pictures. The image that came to symbolize that night's events was a photo of a skull cracked open by a shotgun pellet fired from close range, with the brains spilling out.

Counter-revolution is scarier than revolution, particularly if the revolution is as velvet as it had felt on the roundabout, and so I locked my hotel door as well as I could.

2 THE GREAT SECTARIAN GAME

Bahrain is "pound for pound, man for man, the best ally the
United States has anywhere in the world."

—*William Crowe, former Middle East force commander and
chairman of the Joint Chiefs of Staff[1]*

The mass protests in Tunisia, Egypt, Yemen, and Bahrain, and the
fear that protests could erupt in other Gulf states, put all the Gulf
ruling families at high alert. Small protests in Oman had started in
January 2011, and Saudi Arabia and Kuwait experienced small protests in the following weeks. Regime responses differed from country to country. In Saudi Arabia it was cooptation, repression, and
sectarian rhetoric. The sultan of Oman mixed repression with
reform, initiating some changes immediately. Kuwait became
embroiled in an internal protest movement led largely by Sunnis
and stateless people, the *Bidun*, while Kuwaiti Shia mobilized in
support of the protests in Bahrain and Saudi Arabia. Only Qatar
and the UAE saw no protest movements emerge, but there were
vocal demands for change. In the UAE, the regime's response was
repressive, particularly against human rights activists and the local
branch of the Muslim Brotherhood. Qatar largely deflected political
demands at home by playing a key role in the Arab Spring through

its military involvement in Libya, its support for the Syrian rebels, and particularly through Al-Jazeera, which is funded by Qatar and whose coverage proved key in the ousting of Mubarak of Egypt.

In Bahrain, the Al Khalifa ruling family reacted with repression and contacted their allies in the other Gulf capitals. They got support from the UAE as well as from Qatar, Oman, and Kuwait, but it was several hundred miles more inroad into the Arabian Desert, in the Saudi capital of Riyadh, that their calls were most clearly heard and understood. To the Al Saud ruling family, Bahrain had always been like a part of Saudi Arabia, reliant on the Saudis for its economy and, increasingly, its security. They shared with the Al Khalifa the view of a Shia threat that was somehow inspired or supported by Iran to gain a foothold in the GCC—something they could not allow. What was particularly worrisome to the Saudis was not just the prospect of a constitutional monarchy or real democracy developing in neighboring Bahrain, but the fear that protests in Bahrain could embolden the Shia in the Eastern Province to rise up and demand more rights, a move that could eventually also lead other Saudi citizens to voice their demands. In fact, the Saudi response to the whole Arab Spring, both at home and abroad, was based on the fear that an opposition to the ruling family could emerge that would unite Sunni and Shia. To undermine such a cross-sectarian movement, the ruling family increasingly played on sectarian fears to redirect criticism of domestic politics toward a nationalist rhetoric against Iran and the regime of Bashar al-Assad in Syria.[2]

Turning their eyes to Syria, both the Gulf states and Iran painted the uprising there in a sectarian light, connecting these different conflicts in the eyes of many to a larger sectarian struggle pitting Sunni against Shia (and Shia sects such as the Alawites).[3] To understand the origins of the assumed "Shia threat" or "Shia-phobia"[4] and the Gulf rulers' paranoia about Iranian interference "in internal affairs," as GCC politicians like to put it,[5] one has to look back to the tensions that followed the Iranian Revolution and eventually led to the Saudi-Iranian cold war in the Middle East. Saudi Arabia and Iran are natural geopolitical rivals in the Gulf region because of their size and oil wealth, and their rivalry precedes the 1979 Iranian Revolution, before which both countries were key U.S. allies. Much of their enmity is about geopolitics rather than religion, and reducing it to a Sunni-Shia conflict is too simplistic. Nonetheless both sides in this power struggle are using religion as rhetoric and a foreign policy tool.

After the Iranian Revolution, Iran attempted to rival Saudi Arabia as leader of the community of Muslim believers. Its efforts were largely unsuccessful, and eventually its revolutionary model appealed mainly to the Shia. In the 1980s bilateral relations were extremely tense, not least because Saudi Arabia and other Gulf states bankrolled Iraq in its war against Iran. But after the death of Ayatollah Khomeini in 1989 relations improved. In the 1990s, several of the Gulf states, including Saudi Arabia, had sought to partially defuse tensions with Iran.[6] But with the beginning of the Arab Spring and the threat of protests at home, Saudi Arabia and Bahrain—and by default most other Gulf states—again adopted the sectarian threat narrative as a key discourse to delegitimize popular protests, once again worsening GCC-Iranian relations. This is all to say that it is more useful to look at how religion is used and manipulated by elites to political ends, rather than explain the conflicts plaguing the region solely through references to an age-old schism at the heart of Islam.

Over the past decades sect has become more relevant as a marker of identity in mixed Middle Eastern societies. The Iranian Revolution of 1979 gave hopes to Arab Shia Islamist movements, particularly in the Gulf, Iraq, and Lebanon.[7] It also turned Iran from an ally to a foe of the West and the Arab Gulf monarchies, and led some of them to champion Sunni Islamism against Iranian claims to lead the *umma*, the community of Muslim believers.

The rise to power of Shia Islamist movements in Lebanon and the empowerment of Iraqi Shia after 2003 undermined the long-held assumption that Arab Shia would never play a significant political role and increased the aspirations of Gulf Shia. The sectarian violence in Iraq after the U.S.-led invasion in 2003 harmed sectarian relations across the region. The sectarian Gulf is partly a product of local fallouts related to these larger regional events, the Iranian Revolution and the civil war in Iraq, as well as to the Saudi-Iranian rivalry. But it is also a distinct reaction to the Arab Spring, a conscious and dangerous manipulation of sectarian identities by ruling families and regimes to ensure their political survival.

Because of the interpretation of Islam that dominates Saudi public discourse, the *Wahhabiyya*, Saudi Arabia is the center of doctrinal anti-Shiism. Muhammad Ibn Abd al-Wahhab, a religious scholar from the central Arabian Najd region and founder of the *Wahhabiyya*, established an alliance with the Al Saud dynasty in the mid-eighteenth century. The *Wahhabi* ideology sought to purify Islam and eradicate what was perceived as deviations from the true Islam.[8] A preferred target for their religious zeal was Shia Muslims, particularly those living in the east of the Arabian Peninsula. The Saudi-*Wahhabi* forces repeatedly conquered this fertile area, and it has been part of the Saudi realm since they drove the Ottoman garrison out in 1913.[9] Anti-Shiism remains until this day one of the fundamentals of the *Wahhabi* interpretation of Islam, and of the domestic and foreign policies of the Saudi state. Fatwas and pamphlets against the Shia and other supposedly heretical sects continued to be produced by leading Saudi clerics throughout the twentieth century and were widely disseminated in Saudi Arabia, informing public opinion there. Because of Saudi Arabia's central position in the Muslim world as guardian of the two holy places of Islam, Mecca and Medina, and because of the strength of the Saudi media empire, these anti-Shia edicts gained importance way beyond Saudi Arabia, influencing *salafi-jihadi* groups and fueling sectarian conflict around the world.[10] While many of these edicts focus on doctrinal issues, some target the local Shia communities directly.[11]

The Saudi Twelver Shia are mainly concentrated in Qatif and al-Ahsa. The coastal towns Safwa to the north and Saihat to the south and the island of Tarut, connected to Qatif via a causeway, now form an urban cluster with up to one million people. In the al-Ahsa oasis, located about 140 kilometers inland from Qatif, approximately 180 square kilometers of gardens, palm trees, and villages surround its two main towns, Hofuf and Mubarraz, which nowadays make up one single urban settlement. The population there of about one million is equally divided between Sunnis and Shia. Hofuf used to be the capital of the Eastern Province until 1953, when the capital was moved to the new oil town of Dammam, which was built to accommodate the emerging oil industry and not incidentally separated the American oilmen and other migrants from the older largely Shia settlements. This division between old and new led to underdevelopment in Shia areas, and when I drove around Qatif and the surrounding villages while doing field research there in 2008, some areas resembled slums, with mud roads and decaying city centers.

Historically, the importance of agriculture and landownership in Qatif, and the nature of the other main source of wealth in the region—the pearl trade—led to the development of a prosperous Shia notable class that resided in the old town of Qatif. It was with these notable families that Ibn Saud, the founder of modern Saudi Arabia, struck a deal when he conquered the province in 1913: keep quiet, control your population, and in return you can practice your religion in private.[12]

In the emerging Saudi state, which also conquered the holy cities of Mecca and Medina in 1924–25, the *Wahhabi* clergy oversaw religious affairs and education, and sought to enforce public morality through a religious police. While the eastern region with its oases and ports had always been central to Saudi political and economic calculations, it became even more important with the discovery of oil in the 1930s. The world's largest oil reserves were found in an area largely inhabited by Shia Muslims, whom the

state deemed infidels and suspected of harboring foreign sympa-
thies—narratives during the twentieth century have cast them as
agents for the Ottoman Empire, Iraq, Syria, Nasser's Egypt, the
Soviet Union, or Iran.[13]

Over the years in the nearby oil fields at the ARAMCO oil
company, there remained a glass ceiling for Shia promotion. Many
Shia began to embrace revolutionary ideologies, ranging from
Arab nationalism in its various forms from the 1940s to the 1960s
to Shia Islamism since the 1970s and ultimately the youth-led
activism of 2011. Revolutionary Shia Islamist ideologies spread to
the Eastern Province in the second half of the 1970s, transmitted
by Saudi Shia religious students, who had been studying in Najaf
in Iraq and Qom in Iran. With help from Iraqi and Iranian clerics
based in Kuwait they formed clandestine cells.

These cells were responsible for an uprising by Saudi Shia in
Qatif and the surrounding villages in late 1979—the year of the
Iranian Revolution—and early 1980. The uprising occurred simul-
taneously with the takeover of the Grand Mosque in Mecca by a
group of Sunni rebels on November 20, 1979. This occupation at
the heart of the Muslim world came as a shock to the Saudi
authorities, and the first demonstrations in Qatif only five days
later must have alerted them to the possibility of a rebellion cut-
ting across sectarian lines.[14] The group responsible for the Eastern
Province uprising became known as the *shirazis*. The uprising got
most of its support in the villages, where poverty was widespread
and services were poor, and the negative impacts of the oil industry on the environment could be felt more vividly in the sinking
water levels and poisoned soils that damaged agricultural production. But the uprising was crushed by the Saudi National Guard,
resulting in several dozen casualties.[15]

In the following years, hundreds of young Saudi Shia left the
Eastern Province to join the *shirazi* movement in Iran. After
Kuwait was rocked by a bombing campaign carried out by Shia
Islamist militants, and the *shirazi* wing in Bahrain attempted a

coup there in 1981, the notion of the Shia as a fifth column of Iran, of an enemy within that secretly works to undermine the country, became key in the strategic thinking of Gulf rulers.[16]

Over time though, the Gulf Shia political movements fell out with the Iranians. In 1993, the Saudi *shirazis* reached a deal with King Fahd that granted them a general amnesty and gave them hope that their political, religious, and socioeconomic positions would be improved. While they were now allowed to practice Shia processions in public in majority-Shia areas such as Qatif, anti-Shia incitement and discrimination persisted. Gradually, however, the Shia were surpassed by Sunni Islamists as a main source of opposition to the ruling family. After the first Gulf War, Sunni Islamists known as the *Sahwa* publicly voiced criticism of the ruling family, but their movement was eventually coopted by the regime.[17] Ultimately only after 9/11, with the start of a serious bombing campaign by al-Qaeda in the Arabian Peninsula in 2003, when their former allies turned against the Saudi ruling family, did the Al Saud start to consider al-Qaeda as their main enemy.[18] At times, however, these two threats—the Shia population and Sunni Islamists—continued to be conflated, and Iranian threats to Saudi Arabia remained a key concern for Saudi royals.[19]

When protests began in Bahrain on February 14, 2011, and then spread to the Eastern Province within a matter of days, the Shia once again became the key security threat. Protests in the Eastern Province started on February 17 and continued for several weeks. These early protests by Eastern Province Shia may or may not have scared the ruling family about their own security in Saudi Arabia, but they certainly made the regime even more determined to stop the protests in Bahrain to prevent protests growing in Saudi Arabia. Though the Saudi Shia sought to help the protesters in Bahrain, this might have been counterproductive to their cause. Ali Salman, head of the main Bahraini opposition party al-Wifaq, who tried to broker a deal with the Bahraini crown prince in March 2011, told me, "The timing of the Saudi protests was not very helpful."[20]

Secretary general of al-Wifaq, Ali Salman (C), with a model of the Pearl monument during an opposition gathering in Diraz village, Bahrain, on July 1, 2011. European Pressphoto Agency/Mazen Mahdi.

Fears of follow-up protests in the Eastern Province made Saudi Arabia send troops to Bahrain, in a message addressed to the Saudi Shia and other Saudi citizens who were harboring "heretical" democratic ideas. The Saudi King Abdullah, estimated to be almost ninety years old, is struggling with his health, and was receiving treatment abroad when the Arab Spring threatened to sweep over to Saudi Arabia in early 2011. After his return from abroad in mid-February 2011, the king announced massive spending programs for social security, house loans, health care, religious institutions, and new recruits into the Interior Ministry. The additional spending programs announced in 2011 have a total value of between $120 billion and $130 billion.[21] The additional expenses sent government spending up by 28 percent in 2011 to 804 billion riyals ($214 billion). However, due to high oil prices, government revenue also surged by 51 percent to 1.1 trillion riyals ($270 billion) in the same period.[22]

Many think that during the king's absence, Interior Minister Prince Nayef bin Abd al-Aziz handled state and particularly security affairs, and it is no coincidence that many of the funds announced by the king are channeled through the Interior Ministry.[23] Prince Nayef bin Abd al-Aziz, a hardliner with a zero-tolerance attitude toward political reform and popular protests, became even more powerful when Crown Prince Sultan bin Abd al-Aziz died in October 2011, and Prince Nayef bin Abd al-Aziz was appointed as next in line to the throne. But he too died, in June 2012.

The ruling family has mainly relied on an extremely pervasive security apparatus and massive government handouts of wealth made possible by high oil prices to weather the storm. In addition, the United States in particular stands firmly behind the ruling family, exemplified by the signing on Christmas Eve 2011 of a $29.4 billion arms deal to sell F-15 fighter aircraft to Saudi Arabia.[24] This agreement came weeks after tens of thousands had taken to the streets of the Saudi Eastern Province to protest against the government and mourn the death of several protesters there.

This was yet another sign that the United States sees the Saudi ruling family as key to the two main American interests in the Gulf—oil security and containing Iran.

But the country and the ruling family are not homogeneous entities; it is an absolute monarchy that rules through a narrow power base of close-knit networks of kin and alliances with local elites and the *Wahhabi* religious establishment. Political affairs were largely left to the Al Saud ruling family, whose ranks have swollen to thousands of princes, as long as they did not too openly contradict the religious interpretations of the *Wahhabi* clergy. Senior non-royal businessmen, tribal leaders, and urban notables are part of the entourage of a particular prince, who will help with business deals and political protection.[25] But there are divisions amongst the senior princes about what course Saudi Arabia and indeed the region should take.

The current generation of senior royals, such as King Abdullah and the new crown prince, Salman, are all sons of the founding father of modern Saudi Arabia, King Abd al-Aziz (widely known as Ibn Saud), who ruled until his death in 1953. But they are dying slowly or are becoming too ill to rule. As noted, King Abdullah bin Abd al-Aziz is almost ninety years old and in frail health, and two crown princes have died since 2011. With the appointment of the seventy-seven-year-old Salman bin Abd al-Aziz as the next crown prince in June 2012, the ruling family just delayed the decision about which branch of the next generation of royals it is going to put on the throne. But the fight amongst the new generation of royals for the succession has started in earnest, and Muhammad bin Nayef, Mitaab bin Abdullah, and Bandar bin Sultan are the strongest contenders.[26]

The different factions of the Saudi ruling family are clearly visible in Riyadh, the sprawling Saudi capital of more than five million people in the middle of the desert—a thousand kilometers away from Jeddah on the Red Sea and four hundred kilometers from Qatif and Dammam on the Gulf. Three downtown Riyadh landmarks dotted along the King Fahd Road, Riyadh's main north-south artery, symbolize those different factions. First is Kingdom Tower, a skyscraper built by the flamboyant Saudi business tycoon Prince al-Walid bin Talal. His father is Prince Talal bin Abd al-Aziz, who is the only senior royal who has publicly called for democratic reform and has a long history of political dissent— in the early 1960s he headed the "Free Princes" movement that wanted to create a republic in Saudi Arabia from its exile in Egypt. In the era of King Saud, who reigned from 1953 to 1964, it seemed as if Saudi Arabia could embark on a slightly less autocratic future, but this was brought to a rapid end with the ascension and deposing of King Saud by his half-brother Faisal.[27] A few miles down the King Fahd Road is the Faisaliyya Tower, homage to King Faisal, who ruled from 1964 to 1975. His son Prince Saud al-Faisal is in charge of the Foreign Ministry, and Prince Turki al-Faisal was in charge of the main Saudi intelligence service from 1977 until 2001. Finally there is the rather intimidatingly UFO-shaped Ministry of Interior, once the seat of Prince Nayef, who died in June 2012, and where his son Muhammad bin Nayef, who was in charge of Saudi counterterrorism operations, is now the new minister of interior.

Alarmed that over ten thousand people had signed up on Facebook to participate in a Day of Rage in Saudi Arabia on March 11, 2011, the Ministry of Interior reissued a ban on demonstrations in March 2011. A similar edict followed from the Council of Senior Scholars that is dominated by *Wahhabi* clerics, which argued that demonstrations are contrary to Islamic law. A scholar from the famous al-Azhar University in Cairo subsequently criticized the edict on the grounds that demonstrations can be legitimate against an unjust ruler, but not many within Saudi Arabia dared to do the same.[28] Nevertheless, nationwide calls and online petitions for a constitutional monarchy were circulated and signed by prominent reformists and influential Islamic scholars such as Salman al-Awda.[29] But the Day of Rage passed without major demonstrations in most parts of the country, and in Riyadh only one protester, Khalid al-Juhani, showed up and was arrested in front of the world's media teams and put on trial a year later.[30] Only protesters from the Shia minority in the Eastern Province dared defy the ban. In the evening of Thursday, March 10, one day ahead of the Day of Rage, security forces opened fire on protesters in Qatif.[31]

The Saudi regime played all its cards to keep the people at home: the edict against domestic protests, handouts of wealth, support for the crackdown on protests in Bahrain, and the portrayal in Saudi-owned media of all the protests across the Gulf countries as an Iranian plot carried out with the help of the local Shia populations. The Saudi and Bahraini responses to the Arab Spring effectively created the sectarian Gulf, shielding Gulf ruling families from the legitimate demands of Gulf citizens and putting themselves firmly in line with the West's belligerent rhetoric toward Iran.

In another show of support for the embattled Bahraini regime, Abdul Latif Al Zayani, a Bahraini lieutenant general from a prominent Sunni family, was appointed secretary general of the GCC on April 1, 2011. When I attended a discussion with him at the University of Cambridge in July 2012, Al Zayani, being quizzed about Bahrain, tried to contrast it with the situation in Yemen. He argued that he had personally mediated between the opposition and the regime of Ali Abdullah Salih in Yemen, eventually paving a way for the exit of president Salih. The uprising in Yemen posed a huge challenge to the GCC, above all to Saudi Arabia, which shares a long border with Yemen and was a main backer of the ousted Yemeni president.[32]

In the threat perception of the Saudis then, the sectarian Gulf extended to Yemen, and they were deeply worried about the Houthi movement there, an armed political movement made up of Zaidi Sevener Shia. The short war between Houthi rebels and Saudi Arabia in 2009 and 2010 was accompanied by an anti-Shia discourse and was styled as a holy war against the rejectionists, a common derogatory term for the Shia.[33] Al Zayani made it clear that unlike in Yemen, the GCC did not mediate in Bahrain, but rather sent troops in, because there was "outside interference," which everyone understood to mean Iran.[34]

Saudi Arabia's political leverage in Bahrain has also economic reasons. The Bahraini economy and the state budget are largely dependent on Saudi Arabia. Bahrain derives most of its oil production from the shared Abu Safa offshore field, from which Riyadh grants 50 percent of revenues to Manama. Bahraini refineries are supplied with Saudi crude oil at discounted prices. This amounts to a direct Saudi subsidization of the Bahraini budget.[35] The Bahraini tourism and banking sectors largely depend on Saudi visitors and deposits, and do so even more after the uprising in Bahrain since 2011 led to the departure of many Western banks and a drop in tourist numbers. The sixteen-mile causeway that links Bahrain to the Saudi mainland facilitates mutual trade and travel and is crossed by eighteen million every year.[36] Construction financed by Saudi money started after the Iranian Revolution, when Bahrain's rulers were nervous that a revolution might succeed in Bahrain. Inaugurated in 1986, the causeway has become a vital lifeline for both sides, but one of the purposes of the causeway has always been to enable Saudi troops to roll over in case of a perceived emergency.[37]

Particularly on weekends, thousands of Saudis cross the causeway to get away from the strict moral codes enforced in Saudi Arabia, and many pause at one of the liquor stops, which are conveniently located close to the border, and then move on to one of Manama's bars and nightclubs in the fancy hotels. The Saudis have money to burn that they cannot spend in their country. At the height of the uprising in Bahrain, the Saudi government urged its citizens to stay away from Bahrain for their own safety. One group of Saudis that the Saudi and Bahraini security services were particularly worried about—the Saudi Shia—was outright banned from entering Bahrain, and was turned back by the border guards on the causeway.[38]

For many Saudi Shia, Bahrain and the lands of Qatif and al-Ahsa in the Eastern Province of Saudi Arabia form the mythical homeland of "Ancient Bahrain," a time when the coastal areas along the Gulf between Basra and the peninsula of Qatar were united. By emphasizing the importance of "Ancient Bahrain," Gulf Shia opposition movements have tried to create a nationalist narrative that unifies the mainly Shia inhabitants of Qatif, al-Ahsa, and Bahrain. One of the key factors that mobilized protesters in both Bahrain and the Eastern Province was a sense of *Bahrani* nativism that is key to the cultural memory of the Shia in the Gulf. *Bahrani* is the self-description of the long-standing inhabitants of Bahrain, and the term used in British colonial records to describe them. The *Baharna* are largely Shia.[39]

On Bahrain's Pearl Roundabout one could hear such talk as "We are the original inhabitants of this island" and that the island had been "under the occupation of the Al Khalifa since 1783," the year the Al Khalifa conquered the islands of Bahrain. These are both key components of the nativist argument. And while these narratives are directed against the ruling family, they implicitly also include many other Sunnis and more recent immigrants. Many Bahraini Sunnis arrived together with the Al Khalifa in the late eighteenth and early nineteenth centuries, or were later migrants from Saudi Arabia or the Iranian side of the Gulf coast. Crucially, the Al Khalifa and many Sunni families traced their tribal origins to Najd, the heartland of Saudi Arabia, and the bastion of *Wahhabi* Islam and the Al Saud ruling family.[40] In addition, over the past decades a large number of Sunnis from Arab countries as well as from Pakistan have come to work in various sectors of the state and the economy in Bahrain, not least in the security services, and many of them have been given Bahraini citizenship to increase the percentage of Sunnis on the island. All these groups are excluded in Shia nativist talk, and would therefore be more inclined to cling to the regime, fearing that the nativist rhetoric would have its logical conclusion in the expulsion of some of these groups, particularly those that arrived more recently. This became more pronounced as the dangerous spiral of regime repression and killing of protesters gained pace, and the protesters blamed the violent practices on foreign mercenaries. The mobilization of the Gulf Shia through this nationalist myth, then, limits the mobilization of the Sunnis in Bahrain. It might well be that the propagation of this discourse in discussions, speeches, and on banners on the Pearl Roundabout led many Sunnis, even those that would be sympathetic to major political reforms, to question the motives of the protesters.

These debates about previous settlement, and whether it carries entitlement of political rights, as well as attempts by regimes to cast critics as "foreign agents," are deeply problematic in a region characterized by centuries of seafaring, trade, migration, tribal and imperial conquests, and shifting political alliances. In many ways they are reactions against attempts by post-independence Gulf states to create homogenous nationalist narratives based on a Sunni Arab identity.

3 PEARL ROUNDABOUT

"The people want the fall of the regime!"

"Down with Hamad!"

—*Chants in the Pearl Roundabout, late February 2011*

When I woke up at midday on February 17, 2011, Bahrain had the feeling of being a war zone under siege. I switched on the television; by now Bahrain was all over the English-language channels but there were few if any foreign correspondents in the country, as not many people had anticipated such a turnout on February 14. On Bahrain television—the mouthpiece of the regime—a spokesman for the Ministry of Interior delivered a chilling statement in which he defended the attack on the roundabout and showed knives, swords, and other weapons allegedly found there, as well as wounded police officers. The story seemed to totally contradict what I had witnessed the night before, and what I could gather from people I spoke to and from videos and pictures uploaded on social media. This was the beginning of a media war and disinformation campaign spearheaded by the regime to promote its version of events, a campaign in which Bahrain television and social media were crucial.[1] I had spent several hours on the roundabout the night before, wandering about, stepping in and out of tents, and I did not see a single weapon. Of course, there might have been swords and knives hidden away somewhere, but the idea that these were armed protesters who wanted to spread chaos and had to be removed to restore order, which seemed to be the rationale of the security forces, is absurd.

That same day, February 17, the GCC ministers of foreign affairs gathered in Manama to express their support for the Al Khalifa ruling family. It was a meeting of the reactionaries who were keen to use any means necessary to prevent the spread of revolutionary fervor in the Gulf. However, the press conference did little to purport a sense of normalcy but rather seemed like an influx of foreign allies to an embattled regime shooting its citizens. Indeed, the GCC was founded in 1981 in part to protect the Gulf monarchies against the export of the Iranian revolution, and against subsequent demonstrations by the Gulf Shia. It is the irony of history that Gulf Cooperation Council Roundabout is the official name of what in popular parlance was known as the Pearl Roundabout. Built for the third GCC summit, which was held in Manama in November 1982, it was supposed to celebrate Gulf unity. Now protesters had chosen this very symbol of national and regional identity and political unity and turned it into their symbol of freedom, but had been shot at and were about to return to the roundabout, ready to die.[2]

Shocked by the sudden turn of events, I stayed in the hotel that day, as Bahrain television was urging people to stay away from busy intersections and my friends were not answering their phones. From a jubilant mood, Bahrain had moved to a state of lockdown. The other guests were leaving the hotel, and soon I was almost the only one there. The South-Asian employees at the hotel were scared. When I asked one waiter from Kerala about his opinion, he replied, "It's the Shia, they always make trouble. They don't like the ruling family, and they want to take our jobs. They don't like us, they want all foreigners to leave. But the country works because of us; if we were not here nothing would function."

He was conflating a number of issues that were, however, key. It struck me how many South-Asian workers had come to hate the Shia and associated them with danger, and how they praised, at least publicly and in conversations with foreigners, the ruling family. The spreading of sectarianism and in some cases a *Wahhabi* or *salafi* ideology amongst Muslim migrant workers in the Gulf states also has repercussions in their home countries. When these workers return home, they bring some of the religious beliefs they adopted abroad with them, a problem that has exacerbated sectarian tensions and violence in Afghanistan and Pakistan, both of which have significant Shia minorities.[3]

When the first pro-government demonstrations started a few days later on the other side of town from the Pearl Roundabout, in front of the al-Fatih mosque and along the highways leading to it, many South Asians participated. The name of the mosque means "the Conqueror" in honor of Ahmad al-Fatih, the progenitor of the Al Khalifa ruling family. Not surprisingly, this is seen as an insult by many Bahraini Shia, who see themselves as indigenous Bahrainis, the *Baharna*, conquered by the Al Khalifa.[4] The opposition claimed that the protesters there were either thugs or Indians that were forced to participate. I went to these protests myself, and while there were clearly many Arabs, some of them carrying Saudi and Bahraini flags, I also saw many South Asians. Some of the staff at my hotel and at the many curry and dosa restaurants I ate at in Manama acknowledged that they had been urged by their managers to join in the protests.

But these comments also hint at other issues, namely that Bahraini society is quite diverse, a legacy of Britain's colonial past and the economic boom since the 1970s. Until 2011 the ruling family had ensured freedom of religious worship, which stands in marked contrast to its neighbor Saudi Arabia. There are Hindu temples, Christian churches, a synagogue, and Sunni and Shia mosques, although Bahrain's image of a religiously tolerant society has been severely tarnished by the destruction of several Shia mosques and *hussainiyyas* as part of a government crackdown on dissent in 2011.[5]

While Indians do much of the menial labor in Bahrain, and without them many businesses would indeed cease to function, the anger against foreigners that my waiter mentioned is not mainly directed against the Indians. It is rather directed against another British colonial legacy, the fact that the security services and the police force are to a large degree composed of foreigners, many of whom hail from other former British colonies such as Pakistan.

Amongst the Shia, and also amongst the liberal and oppositional Sunnis, there is a broad conviction that the Bahraini regime has pursued a strategy of naturalization of Sunnis from various backgrounds (particularly Pakistan but also Saudi Arabia, Syria, Jordan, and so on) in order to change the sectarian demographic of the country and create a loyalist citizen base in the event of mass protests against the monarchy as witnessed in 2011.[6] In the wake of the uprising in Syria, Bahrain reportedly planned to give citizenship to up to five thousand Sunni Syrian refugees.[7] Yet another legacy of colonialism are the British advisers and officers that remained key in the Bahraini security forces.[8]

After the horror in the early morning of February 17, Crown Prince Salman bin Hamad Al Khalifa appeared on television on February 18 to offer to start a dialogue with the opposition, urging all sides to remain calm.[9] Fearing the protests would get out of control, King Hamad had announced that the government would allow peaceful demonstrations and would punish no one for participating in them. His son the crown prince then opened secret talks with al-Wifaq and six other legal opposition groups about organizing a public dialogue on political reform. This seeming normalization, and the sense that it was safe to go to the roundabout, made people hopeful that their demands would be heard.

On February 19, security forces withdrew from the Pearl Roundabout and allowed protesters back. At first I was a bit hesitant to return, as just two days earlier people had beetn shot there, but when I went to the roundabout a day later, on February 20,

Protesters wave flags and celebrate after reaching the Pearl Roundabout in Manama, Bahrain, on February 19, 2011. European Pressphoto Agency/Mazen Mahdi.

the mood was jubilant, while political demands had risen. There were now more tents and makeshift infrastructure than on February 16, and people were installing themselves for the long haul. They erected a large podium for speakers, where politicians and social activists but also ordinary people spoke, and which became a kind of speaker's corner for Bahraini society over the coming month. The slogans had become more radical. Instead of "The people want the reform of the regime," thousands now shouted, "The people want the fall of the regime," the same slogan as in Tunisia and Egypt. Occasionally, one could also hear or read references against the ruling family itself, for example those calling for "death to Al Khalifa."

Gradually, some people started to enforce Islamic mores, setting up distinct areas for women that were surrounded by the fences left by the security forces after their crackdown only days earlier. Apparently al-Wifaq, the largest Shia opposition movement, had ordered this separation, and it stood in marked contrast to the mix between sexes and ages and the rather anarchic spirit of the two days on the roundabout before the crackdown.

Amongst the earliest demands of protesters was the immediate release of political prisoners arrested in the months before the uprising, and particularly during a crackdown on opposition leaders, bloggers, and human rights activists in 2010.[10] Many were released, and they immediately joined the crowds in the roundabout before then heading on to *al-Wasat*, the only opposition newspaper in Bahrain, to have their pictures taken and tell their stories.

I drove out to the offices of *al-Wasat*, located in a large factory-style building on Budaya Highway, the highway that leads to a number of the Shia villages. Inside, the mood was jubilant. Every day the newspaper's pages were filled with stories of released prisoners, of their experience of beatings and torture, and their joy to be free and part of the "revolution." In the hallway I met Ali Abdulemam, a prominent blogger roughly my age who had been arrested in August 2010 for his Internet activism. Immediately after his release, he went to the protests to take center stage, and shortly after went into hiding to avoid being rearrested. He was later tried in absentia and sentenced to fifteen years in prison.[11]

Mansoor al-Jamri, the editor-in-chief of *al-Wasat* and a key Bahraini Shia intellectual from a prominent religious family, sat in his large office, extremely tired but optimistic about where the political situation was heading. Al-Jamri's father had been one of the main Shia clerics in Bahrain and one of the leaders of the uprising in the 1990s, and he therefore enjoyed an important social standing. Like everyone else he had hardly slept since the protests erupted on February 14, as events had moved so quickly. He was involved in the secret negotiations between the opposition and the Bahraini crown prince, but argued that it was difficult to convince the more radical opposition and the youth groups that sought the overthrow of the regime that they should negotiate. He also criticized a particular group of protesters, the *shirazis*: "The *shirazis* are not key in the protests, they represent a minority, but their political views and activities in the roundabout are divisive and—together with Hadi al-Mudarrisi's speeches from abroad— may well lead to a confrontation with the government."[12]

When I returned to the roundabout, it struck me how the *shirazi* activists had set up their own large screen with a width of several meters, on which they were projecting *shirazi* television channels from Kuwait and Iraq. Though the *shirazi* movement is rather peripheral to the wider world of Shia political movements, they are well organized and have their own media.

After the death of the movement's spiritual leader, Muhammad Mahdi al-Shirazi, in 2001, the *shirazi* movement split into follow- ers of the *marji'iyya* of his brother, Sadiq al-Shirazi, and followers of the *marji'iyya* of his nephew Muhammad Taqi al-Mudarrisi. A *marji' al-taqlid* is literally a reference point for emulation, some- one that is qualified through his learning and probity to be fol- lowed in all points of religious practice and law by the generality of Shia Muslims. While Sadiq al-Shirazi vowed to continue in the footsteps of his brother, and adopted an increasingly nonconfrontational approach toward the Gulf governments, the more politically minded decided to follow the *marji'iyya* of Muhammad Taqi al-Mudarrisi and his brother Hadi al-Mudarrisi, which started to be called the *mudarrisiyya* by its followers.[13]

Some of those who switched to the *mudarrisiyya* are parts of the *shirazi* party in Bahrain—Amal—and some are clerics in Saudi Arabia, such as Muhammad al-Habib and Nimr al-Nimr. Al-Nimr was the only cleric who backed the protests in his native village of Awwamiyya from the beginning and called for the downfall of the Saudi ruling family. Speculations abound over whether the al-Mudarrisis indeed urged their followers in Saudi Arabia and Bahrain to move against their governments, or whether this was a local decision by the youth and some clerics, who felt that the time was ripe for change.

A number of *shiraziyya* and *mudarrisiyya* television channels exist in Kuwait and Iraq, including Ahlulbait television, whose name is a reference to the "family of the house of the Prophet," that is, the descendants of the Prophet, or imams, that are revered by Shia Muslims. On that channel, the former leader of the *shirazi* movement in Bahrain, Hadi al-Mudarrisi, started to give daily speeches about the situation in Bahrain. Al-Mudarrisi is originally a descendant of a clerical family of Iranian-Iraqi origin. He had come to Bahrain in the early 1970s, where he set up the Bahraini branch of the *shiraziyya*, later to be known as the Islamic Front for the Liberation of Bahrain (IFLB),[14] and was even given Bahraini citizenship in 1974. But after protests in 1979 he was expelled and declared persona non grata. The IFLB was involved in a coup attempt in 1981, and its members were thereafter only active underground or abroad. But they and the other clandestine opposition groups were also allowed to come back as part of the reform program of the new King Hamad in 2001, and they created a political organization, Amal, which officially had no links with Hadi al-Mudarrisi anymore.

So to see his face on a large screen in the heart of Manama was quite a surprise. The other political groups, particularly the largest Shia opposition group, al-Wifaq, rejected all accusations of foreign links and tried not to be instrumentalized by foreign Shia actors. But the *shirazis* had put a screen up for their former leader, on which he was speaking out in the harshest ways against the Al Khalifa ruling family and, slowly, also against the Saudi ruling family. Thereby, al-Mudarrisi and his Bahraini supporters were giving the hardliners in the regime evidence to cast this as a foreign plot. After all, an Iranian-Iraqi cleric with a long history of political subversion in the Gulf was urging the protesters to rise up via satellite television. And indeed, once the Bahraini government and its supporters pushed the sectarian narrative in its counterrevolution, the image of Hadi al-Mudarrisi was often a scapegoat.[15] The regime tried very hard to link the 2011 protests to the 1981 coup plot, going as far as reading for hours on Bahrain television from clandestine publications from the 1980s to make the point that Iran together with the IFLB had plotted the 2011 "coup" for three decades. While in Bahrain in May 2011 I saw several shows on Bahrain TV during which a presenter read from IFLB publications and from an account of the 1981 coup attempt written by a former member of the group[16] to try to make that claim. The regime even withdrew the citizenship of thirty-one Bahrainis in November 2012 under the pretext that they were still members of the IFLB, even though they were clearly activists form other Shia groups and not affiliated with the *shirazis*.[17] Indeed, while former IFLB activists do not deny that they attempted a coup in 1981, they argue that they did this without the knowledge of the Iranian leadership and that it angered the Iranians responsible for foreign policy.[18]

The less political *shirazis*, however, did not endorse the views of Hadi al-Mudarrisi. When I asked the son of Sadiq al-Shirazi, Ahmad al-Shirazi, about the role of the al-Mudarrisi brothers and their harsh stance against the Gulf rulers, he emphasized diplomatically that he and his father—the effective head of the *shirazi* movement—were against the oppression of people wherever they might be, including in Bahrain. However, regarding the al-Mudarrisi, he replied that "we disagree with them on some issues."[19] For a public reply of a cleric this was quite blunt, and reflected the deep divisions within the movement, to the extent that it no longer makes sense to refer to all of them as *shirazis*, even though the term is still applied colloquially.

A final example of this is the owner of a *shirazi* bookshop in the heart of the old town of Manama, in the lanes that host the old Shia mourning houses and mosques. Some of these mourning houses, which are locally referred to as the Iranian mourning houses, openly displayed pictures of Ayatollah Ruhollah Khomeini and Ayatollah Ali Khamenei, the supreme leader of Iran, and in February 2011 the shop for religious souvenirs next to the *shirazi* bookshop was still selling mugs with the picture of the two Iranian Ayatollahs, whom many in the ruling family see as arch-enemies of Bahrain. A 2006 American diplomatic cable describes a luncheon with the Bahraini King Hamad, who argued that "as long as Khamenei has the title of Commander-in-Chief, Bahrain must worry about the loyalty of Shia who maintain ties and allegiance to Iran" and that this was the reason why Shia were not represented in the military leadership of Bahrain.[20]

In May 2011, two months after the crackdown on protesters, the mugs had disappeared. But in February 2011 the contrast between the apolitical owner of the religious bookshop and his more political counterparts with the Khamenei mugs and on the Pearl Roundabout could not have been more pronounced. A few days into the uprising, the *shirazi* bookseller had not even been to the Pearl Roundabout and argued that the Shia should just be content with the religious freedom they have here and live their lives quietly, without being involved in politics. Otherwise, Bahrain would end up like Iraq, and that was the worst possible outcome. He had just come back from a trip to Karbala, where he had visited the shrines revered by Shia Muslims and had bought books. He was appalled by the lack of security in Iraq, and preferred Bahrain, where the Shia had until 2011 enjoyed more religious freedoms than elsewhere, as symbolized in the yearly Muharram celebrations in front of his shop. So while the apolitical and religiously minded wing of the *shirazis* largely refrained from being involved in politics, the more political side, and the side associated with the al-Mudarrisis, who had become very weak in post-Saddam Iraq, wanted to use this opportunity to reassert themselves in the Gulf.

This brings us back to the question of who was driving the protests and whether these protests were, as the regime later tried to make the whole world believe, a plot inspired and directed by sectarian agents of Iran or Lebanese Hizbullah. The initial protests, and the taking of the Pearl Roundabout, were very much the product of a group of *shabab*, or young men. In the days before February 14, youth groups in the various villages and quarters around Bahrain organized online, particularly via Facebook, and planned to head to the Pearl Roundabout. The large turnout on that day surprised even them.[21] But once they had conquered the roundabout, the Shia Islamist movements joined them with their followers and their organizational support.

In the evening of February 24, I returned to the roundabout. As I walked around, the political carnival was in full swing. Speakers tried to capture the attention of the crowd. Large tents had been set up in the area surrounding the roundabout, and protesters were occupying ever more territory.

I met up with a cleric whom I had gotten to know earlier in a bookshop in one of the Shia villages outside of Manama. He was 'ajam, a Shia of Iranian origin, and often said "yes" in the Persian way instead of the Arabic affirmative. He was active in publishing and had written a few books about local history—a popular pastime amongst Shia clerics and intellectuals—but he had also been involved in Shia opposition movements. He wanted to introduce me to his group of people, and wanted me to speak to a few of the *shabab* so that I would get a better understanding of what was going on. He took me a few hundred yards away from the round-about to a large tent, under which a dozen men were sitting and sipping tea. Their views were, as those of almost all the people on the roundabout, very critical of the regime and the ruling family. When I asked them which group they belonged to they responded, Hizbullah.

This was quite a statement to make. The pro-Iranian Hizbullah trend, locally known as *Khat al-Imam*, referring to followers of the line of Imam Khomeini, is one of the strands of political Shia Islam that had been prevalent in the Gulf for decades. There is a huge debate in Bahrain and the wider Gulf as to whether an Iranian-inspired or sponsored Hizbullah exists in Bahrain and whether it was involved in the protests. The regime and its media would usu-ally blame all the protests on the local Hizbullah cells, and hint at involvement from Lebanese Hizbullah and Iran. The Shia political parties, including al-Wifaq, would never acknowledge that Hizbul-lah exists in Bahrain, and would argue that al-Wifaq is a local party. The truth is, however, somewhere in between, as my encoun-ter with several Hizbullahis at the Pearl Roundabout proved.

There are three main trends of political Islam amongst Arab Shia: al-Dawa, Hizbullah, and the *shirazis*. Al-Dawa was founded by Muhammad Baqir al-Sadr in Iraq, and expanded particularly to Kuwait and Bahrain, but never became strong amongst the Shia in Saudi Arabia. After the fall of Saddam, a branch of the Dawa Party became the dominant party in Iraqi politics, with Iraq's Prime Minister Nuri al-Maliki at its head.[22] The Hizbullah trend emerged in some Gulf countries out of al-Dawa, particularly in Kuwait, and incorporates those Shia Muslims that follow the supreme leader of the Islamic Republic of Iran as their spiritual guide, formerly Ayatollah Khomeini and since his death in 1989, Ayatollah Khamenei. Given the bad relations between the Gulf states and Iran, and the almost paranoid fear of Gulf rulers of Iranian subversion, it is particularly this Hizbullah trend that is worrying the regimes, and that is looked upon with suspicion.[23] Up to half the cadres and supporters of al-Wifaq come from the Hizbullah strand, while the other half come from al-Dawa, in addition to a number of supporters who do not come from either of those. If one directly asks Wifaqis, they will respond that yes, I am originally Hizbullah or yes, I am originally al-Dawa. Clerics certainly do play a key role in al-Wifaq. Its general secretary, Ali Salman, the assistant general secretary, Hussayn al-Dayhi, and the spiritual guide, Isa Qasim, are prominent clerics. But that does not mean that al-Wifaq's agenda is firmly in line with Iranian regional ambitions, or that all of al-Wifaq is Hizbullah.[24]

The cleric who did most of the talking in the tent claimed that he had been imprisoned in the 1990s for membership in Hizbullah. And he would still argue that he defended the ideals of Hizbullah, that is, that society should be led by clerics, that their spiritual leader was Ayatollah Khamenei, and that the group stood in the spirit of Ayatollah Khomeini. The Hizbullah networks are characterized by adherence to *wilayat al-faqih*, the guardianship of the jurisprudent, which is the political system of Iran.

This was classic Hizbullah ideology, as proclaimed by Lebanese Hizbullah and its sister organizations in Iraq and the Gulf. However, and he was quite clear about that, he did not want Bahrain to be part of Iran, or to have an Iranian-style system in Bahrain. This would not work, he argued, since Bahrain was not a homogenous country, and the Iranians did not know what was best for Bahrain. Then he introduced me to a few young men, who had been involved in the storming of the roundabout and were loosely affiliated with his group. But they argued that the majority of the youths did not have a political affiliation, and they were trying to set up a group that would represent the youth interests from all different political backgrounds. That proved to be quite a difficult task, as there were diverging views, and particularly the established parties such as al-Wifaq tried to prevent the more radical currents amongst the youth from prevailing.

Tens of thousands of protesters march in front of Bahrain Financial Harbour on March 4, 2011, in Manama, Bahrain. European Pressphoto Agency/Mazen Mahdi.

This was indeed one of the main outcomes of the Arab uprisings, not just in Bahrain but across the region: the empowerment of loosely organized youth movements with no coherent leadership vis-a-vis more established opposition parties. And this was the impression I gathered from talking to young Bahrainis, both men and women, on the Pearl Roundabout. These young activists have played a key part in organizing the protests and then conveying information to protesters and to the outside world, using social media, online forums, and other websites, as well as contacts with foreign journalists. On the roundabout, talk was everywhere of the "14 February Youth," and several similar names were written in graffiti on the wall or mentioned to me in discussions.

Eventually these various youth groups, all claiming to have participated in the initial storming of the Pearl Roundabout on February 14, formed the Coalition of Youth of the 14 February Revolution (hereafter 14 February Coalition), a decentralized umbrella organization for the various anti-monarchy youth groups. The nucleus for the coalition was laid between the crackdown on February 17 and the return to the roundabout on February 19.[25] The 14 February Coalition shared many characteristics with some of the youth groups that started the revolution in Egypt, mainly the April 6 Youth Movement, and the Bahraini and other Gulf activists were in touch with the Egyptians before and after the fall of Mubarak.[26]

The initial protests in February and March 2011 were largely peaceful. Until a couple of days before the February 14 protests, youths were still burning tires in the Shia villages to protest against the government. But as they saw the success of the peaceful masses in Tunisia and Egypt, and as they reached the Pearl Roundabout, they understood that peaceful mass protest was more effective than the small-scale violence that had characterized protests in previous decades. As Muhammad al-Maskati, the founder of the Bahrain Youth Society for Human Rights, told me over lunch in May 2011, he and others had urged the youths for several years to embrace peaceful protests.[27]

Meanwhile on the roundabout, the more confrontational wing of the political opposition established a "coalition for a republic" on March 7 that sought to overthrow the monarchy. The coalition was announced by three unlicensed political societies (Haqq, al-Wafa, and the Bahrain Islamic Freedom Movement[28]) and vowed to work closely together with the 14 February Coalition.[29] Haqq leader Hasan Mushayma proclaimed on the Pearl Roundabout, "This tripartite coalition adopts the choice of bringing down the existing regime in Bahrain and establishing a democratic republican system."[30]

The 14 February Coalition also wanted to overthrow the current regime, without however specifying the type of government that should follow. This should be decided in a popular referendum after the fall of the current regime.[31] To achieve this aim, the 14 February Coalition wanted to spread protests beyond the roundabout, and on March 11, 2011, organized a march toward Riffa, an upper-class and largely Sunni neighborhood, where the royal court is located and where many royals live. This was seen as an affront by the ruling family and many other Sunnis. Protesters then moved to block the roads surrounding the Pearl Roundabout, particularly in front of the Bahrain Financial Harbour, a skyscraper complex that was a prestige project of Bahrain's economic development and is allegedly owned by the prime minister.

So while the Bahraini crown prince was negotiating secretly with the seven licensed opposition societies including the Shia bloc al-Wifaq to bring Bahrain closer to a constitutional monarchy, the 14 February Coalition and the "coalition for a republic" were raising the stakes. The pro-regime propaganda machine quickly argued that the coalition had called for an "Islamic republic," and many Sunnis in the Gulf still believe this, even though the coalition never used that term. The Bahraini crown prince seemed to have offered significant democratic reforms and a much greater say for the people, including the Shia, in government.[32] But as rumors about the negotiations reached the roundabout, where the mood was swiftly changing in favor of a republic instead of a constitutional monarchy, some of the revolutionaries criticized al-Wifaq. And hardliners in the ruling family surrounding Prime Minister Prince Khalifa bin Salman Al Khalifa, whose position was personally threatened by the protesters, secretly worked on a different solution to the "problem" of mass protests for democratic change. Their solution was to foment sectarianism.

4   COUNTER-REVOLUTION

"An external plot has been fomented for 20 to 30 years for the ground to be ripe for subversive designs. I here announce the failure of the fomented subversive plot."

—*King Hamad Al Khalifa, speaking to officers of the Peninsula Shield Force, March 21, 2011*[1]

"The rulers of Bahrain claimed that Iran is involved in the events of Bahrain. This is a lie. No, we do not interfere. . . . If we had interfered, the conditions would have been different in Bahrain."

—*Ayatollah Ali Khamenei, supreme leader of the Islamic Republic of Iran, Friday prayer in Tehran, February 3, 2012*[2]

By my next visit to Bahrain in May 2011, the country was a profoundly different place. On March 14, 2011, Saudi troops had crossed the causeway between the Eastern Province and Bahrain, later followed by policemen from the UAE. They were nominally part of the Peninsula Shield Force, the common GCC force that had hardly been used before.[3] Even though the Gulf regimes claim that the foreign forces went straight to the barracks and were not involved in policing, large parts of the opposition were affronted by the deployment of foreign forces made up entirely of Sunnis to stifle the protests. For many Bahrainis, particularly many Shia, Bahrain has been under effective occupation since that day. A part of the population, many of them Sunnis, saw the influx of foreign troops as saviors, and the regime ensured that not just the Saudi tanks on the streets made it feel like a province of Saudi Arabia. Outside the Bahraini parliament, Saudi flags and huge posters of Saudi Arabia's King Abdullah were put up, and T-shirts and pins describing Saudi Arabia as the "Kingdom of Humanitarianism" were sold at street corners.

The troops supposedly were invited by the king of Bahrain under a defense agreement of the Gulf Cooperation Council, although it is likely that the decision was reached by the right wing in the ruling family together with hawkish figures in the Saudi ruling family, such as the now deceased Interior Minister Prince Nayef bin Abd al-Aziz Al Saud. Several members of the Bahraini ruling family are opposed to major political changes: Prime Minister Khalifa bin Salman Al Khalifa, against whom tens of thousands were protesting, as well as a branch of the Al Khalifa that is known as the Khawalids. The Khawalids stem from a different branch of the Al Khalifa family than the king and the crown prince—they are descendants of Khalid bin Ali Al Khalifa and feel disenfranchised in the succession to the throne. They were sidelined by the British but have regained increasing importance over the past decade, and they now hold key positions: Royal Court Minister Khalid bin Ahmad Al Khalifa; the commander of the Bahrain Defense Forces, Khalifa bin Ahmad Al Khalifa; and Minister of Justice Khalid bin Ali Al Khalifa are all Khawalids.[4]

These hardliners were very displeased with the concessions that the Bahraini crown prince seemed to offer to the opposition, and therefore the Saudi troops came in to stop that process. The pictures of the tanks and armored personnel carriers rolling over the causeway that links the two countries went around the world and

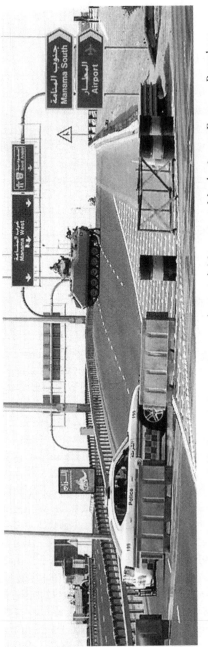

A Bahrain police car and an army tank block a main intersection near the capital, Manama, on March 16, 2011. European Pressphoto Agency/Mazen Mahdi.

marked the end of the first, very optimistic stage of the Arab Spring. From now on, the counter-revolutionary forces would fight back, and no dictator was to fall or step down without months or years of bloodshed. Even beyond the Gulf, "Saudi Arabia emerged as the center of counterrevoution, spreading wealth and political support to conservative regimes across the region."[5]

Martial law followed, called a "state of national safety," together with mass arrests, a partial curfew, a ban on rallies, and a general crackdown on those seen as sympathetic to the protests. The strategic importance of Bahrain to the GCC, and the Saudi fears that protests might spill over into the Eastern Province, had prompted the Saudi ruling family to act. Bahrain was seen as the weakest link of all the Gulf States, susceptible to popular pressure and interference from abroad, and in particular the Saudis were afraid that Iran would profit from any change in government in Bahrain.

I had agreed to work for the International Crisis Group because I felt that the sectarianism emanating from Bahrain might lead to a conflict in the region, and I was shocked that many of the people I had met on my previous trip were now either dead, in jail, or in exile. To put it briefly, Bahrain in 2011 was for me and for many others a crash course in power politics. Social media are a good way to organize revolutions, sometimes. But guns and tanks are very effective tools to stop revolutions, particularly if, unlike in Libya and Egypt, the soldiers are loyal to the regime and international pressure on the regime is limited.

The country now seemed, effectively, to be at war. The men with the machine guns at checkpoints, and those manning the guns on tanks, hid their faces. They wore ski masks, and this was paramount to what Bahrain had become, how its social fabric had been ripped apart. In this tiny nation of just over six hundred thousand citizens, those with guns were afraid that one day they might be held accountable. The fact that they lived in villages and settlements whose entrances were guarded did not seem to make them feel much safer.

Driving across the island and entering Shia and Sunni villages, I became aware of how deeply intertwined urban geography; political protest; and ethnic, sectarian, and class divisions were. But urban planning was key, too. Large-scale street protests, even though organized online, relate to the city or the village structures that shape the daily lives of people. One of the key challenges in all the Arab Spring protests was the need to overcome the urban planning that limited the kinds of public spaces that could facilitate protests. Much of the urban space had been crisscrossed by highways, traffic intersections, and other obstacles. Some cities in the Middle East do have major public spaces, usually a legacy of colonial rule or war, such as in Beirut, which did see a youth-led protest movement in 2006 but not in 2011. Downtown Cairo does have some parks and boulevards, but Tahrir Square, even though nominally a square, is an extremely busy traffic roundabout. The same is true in Bahrain: the center of the Pearl Roundabout was actually quite small, and people would normally not go there because of the mass of cars driving around the roundabout. In addition, a major suburban highway passes over a bridge just next to the roundabout, giving the area even less the feeling and appeal of a public space and making it particularly adverse to any sort of gathering. There was nothing resembling a Tiananmen Square, or a Parliament Square, or even a large park in the city center where people could have gathered. But protesters turned this element of control upside down, and from the first day after youth protesters had stormed the roundabout, they parked cars in the vicinity of the roundabout, thereby physically expanding the zone of protest exponentially. The Pearl Roundabout lies right in the middle of the financial center; the old city of Manama; and the Shia villages Dayh, Sanabis, and Barhama. These villages are referred to as the "steadfastness triangle" due to their central role in the protests, and they have over the years become one urban cluster and form de-facto suburbs of Manama. What was new in 2011 was that these mass protest movements had come to the city and were not confined to the villages anymore.[6] Shia villages had for decades seen frequent protests, and particularly the nightly burning of tires on roads. They had also seen much of the violence in the 1990s uprising. After the crackdown on the Pearl Roundabout then, the geography of protests returned to the villages, where ever since there have been weekly and sometimes daily protests. These villages have a distinctively Shia feel to them, with Shia mosques and mourning houses, black banners praising Imam Hussayn, and decorations with light bulbs hanging across streets—remnants of Shia celebrations during Muharram. The walls are filled with anti-regime graffiti, ranging from "The people want the fall of the regime" to "Down with Hamad" and "Death to Al Khalifa." Each of these villages has its own network of local activists and, increasingly, youth groups, and each village has an online presence, be it through discussion forums, websites, or social media sites. This is linked to the density of smartphones and social media usage, which across the Gulf is one of the highest in the world. On these online resources protests are advertised; local news, including the arrests of protesters, is publicized; and people share—for example—experience with checkpoints, tear gas attacks, and the like. If the police enter a village, then residents quickly know through the social media feed of the "Free people of Village X or Y."

The villages are divided pretty clearly, with some mainly Sunni and some Shia, and this is also the case in the Saudi Eastern Province. Sectarian divisions are entrenched through landholding patterns, urban development, and policing. As part of the counter-revolutionary measures, the security forces in Bahrain and the Eastern Province set up checkpoints at the entrances of Shia villages, a practice that has continued ever since. Mahazza village on Sitra island in Bahrain was under a literal siege from the security forces for several weeks in late 2012.[7] Conflicts at these checkpoints, which made traveling in the area very difficult, frequently led to skirmishes. After several Shia youths were shot in November 2011 at checkpoints in the Eastern Province, protests there intensified.

Within the villages security forces operate in a very hostile environment. They usually come in to break up a protest, fire tear gas and rubber bullets, arrest a few people, and then leave, and as soon as they are out of the village, people come back on the streets again. These protests are filmed, and videos are uploaded to the Internet very quickly, spreading news and a sense of continuing protests around the world to those who want to know. This village structure therefore ensures that the uprising can go on almost indefinitely and cannot be crushed totally, as protests in the village remain an option. But what counts for the Bahraini regime is that as long as protests are confined to the villages and do not spread to the city center, these protests are acceptable, as they are much less visible to the Sunnis of Bahrain and international mainstream media face difficulties covering the events. There are countless stories of how foreign journalists were turned back at the airport or prevented from going to the village protests, or in some cases were even being attacked and arrested after filming there.[8]

What was pervasive particularly amongst the Shia was a shocking sense of fear. Everyone was afraid for their and their families' lives. Even relatively wealthy Shia community leaders have been targeted. Abd al-Karim Fakhrawi was the owner of a publishing house, a bookstore chain, and a construction firm, and was one of the founders of the newspaper *al-Wasat*. He was an *'ajam*, a Shia of Iranian origin, and many in Bahrain believe that he was chosen because of his origin and in order to threaten the *'ajam*, who make up around 10 percent of Bahraini Shia.[9] He was arrested on April 3, 2011, when he went to inquire why police had surrounded one of his relatives' homes the night before. On April 11 he died of kidney and heart failure after being tortured.[10]

In May I went to the largest Fakhrawi bookshop in the Shia village of Jidd Hafs to find it empty but for the Indian shopkeeper. Fakhrawi had published dozens of books about the history of Bahrain, and I gathered as many as I could. I bought a dead man's books from an Indian shopkeeper who could neither speak Arabic nor read the Arabic book titles, who probably did not know much about the conflict raging in Bahrain, and who was incited by the English-language government press to hate Shia Muslims and to believe that they would expel or otherwise hurt foreign workers in Bahrain if the Shia ever came to power. I did not ask for a discount.

The crackdown also encompassed the newspaper *al-Wasat*, of which, as mentioned, Fakhrawi was one of the founders. Its editor-in-chief and mastermind, Mansoor al-Jamri, was also fearing for his life when I met him again in May 2011. The memories of him being editor of one of the most popular newspapers, being able to travel to conferences abroad and meeting with senior members of the ruling family, seemed distant. After the crackdown in March 2011, he had been forced to resign as editor-in-chief on April 3.[11] He was afraid to meet in public, and had been told to stay away from foreigners. So we met clandestinely. I had to follow him to his car in an underground parking lot, where we dismantled our mobile phones, which, like the phones of everyone else remotely involved with politics in Bahrain, were being monitored around the clock with the help of software provided by Western companies.[12] After we arrived at a house on the outskirts of one of the Shia villages, he told me about the horrors of the crackdown, of the disappearances, of the beatings, the killings, and how his acquaintances in the ruling family and the regime had let him down.

All the opposition groups had been hit hard by the crackdown, but some were targeted more than others. Al-Wifaq in some ways retained a special status, as it presented the moderate end of the opposition and the Americans saw al-Wifaq as key to any political settlement. Nevertheless, as the crackdown intensified, al-Wifaq was also punished. Its general secretary, Ali al-Salman, was shot in the head with a tear gas canister from close range at a protest, while two former al-Wifaq MPs were stripped of their citizenship.[13]

But those that had called for the downfall of the regime, and activists from the leftist group Wa'ad, an Arab Nationalist group made up of both Sunni and Shia, were targeted in particular. The arrest on March 17 of the Sunni Ibrahim Sharif, secretary general of Wa'ad, by a commando group of masked special forces serves to

The secretary general of Wa'ad, Ibrahim Sharif, holding a placard calling for the fall of the government at a protest in Bahrain on March 6, 2011. Mazen Mahdi.

illustrate this point. I had met him on the roundabout in February, where he had given fiery speeches in support of the protest movement and urging Sunni-Shia unity. In the meantime, the Wa'ad headquarters had become a meeting point for the professionals and intellectuals of the liberal and secular opposition in Bahrain. When I returned to Europe, I saw footage online of the Wa'ad headquarters after it had been ransacked by a pro-regime mob. Large parts of where I had sat with old Arab Nationalists, Nasserists, and communists and read the Bahraini newspapers were burned to the ground. Ibrahim Sharif detailed his torture in prison in letters smuggled out of prison and posted online.[14]

If these kinds of people were seen as a threat to the Bahraini regime and treated in that way, it was painful to imagine what they were doing to young protesters when the security forces and pro-regime mobs stormed their houses in their nightly raids.

Wa'ad then got its license as a political society revoked, but when I visited Farida Ghulam, a leader of Wa'ad and the wife of Ibrahim Sharif, in May 2011, she and the political leadership of the society were intent on standing their ground. Shortly afterward, Sharif was sentenced to five years by a special security court.

Contrary to the imprisoned Islamist leaders, with whom foreign embassies found it difficult to bond, Sharif was even known in some Western capitals. By arresting him the Bahraini regime lost some goodwill abroad but managed to scare those Sunnis willing to side with the opposition. Other pro-opposition Sunnis were also targeted. When I went to interview Munira Fakhro, another Sunni leader of Wa'ad and a professor of sociology at the University of Bahrain, in May 2011 there were still signs of the petrol bombs that had been thrown at her house by pro-regime mobs in order to scare her. Fakhro stems from a wealthy merchant family, but even with her connections and public standing one could be targeted—being a Sunni did not help. Indeed she reiterated that the regime was most afraid of people like her embracing the protests, those that are well-educated, wealthy, and anti-sectarian. And she argued that the divisions between loyalists and opponents, and between Sunni and Shia, were deeper than ever before and would take decades to heal, even if a true reconciliation were to take place now.

Ibrahim Sharif's sentence was upheld in early September 2012 by a civilian court, after he had initially been convicted by a military court, as were the sentences against nineteen other Bahraini opposition leaders, including the leadership of Haqq, al-Wafa, and the shirazis. Eight of these activists are jailed for life, including the prominent human rights activist and former *shirazi* political opposition activist Abd al-Hadi al-Khawaja. He staged a 110-day hunger strike in 2012 that received worldwide attention but did not lead to his release.[15] The opposition leaders and human rights activists lost their final appeal in early January 2013, and they will probably have to spend long years in jail.[16]

Another human rights activist who became a political activist was Nabil Rajab, who in May 2011 seemed like the "last man standing." Nabil had co-founded the Bahrain Center for Human Rights with Abd al-Hadi al-Khawaja. He now acted as its head and was an interlocutor for international and regional human rights organizations, including Human Rights Watch. Because he stemmed from a wealthy Shia family with generally good relations with the ruling family, and was a secularist, his activism and his international contacts posed a problem for the regime and he was not arrested in the first crackdown that targeted the other opposition leaders and human rights activists after the arrival of Saudi troops in mid-March 2011. When I interviewed him at home in May 2011, he was defiant, arguing that he would rather die or go to prison than give up his cause. While we were sitting in his living room, there was a constant coming and going of victims of torture or police abuse, or relatives of political prisoners who dropped in and told him their stories. Rajab led small unlicensed protests throughout 2011 and 2012 and continued to criticize the ruling family on Twitter and in interviews with foreign media. After traveling abroad, and appearing on the BBC's HARDtalk and Julian Assange's TV show, he was arrested at Manama airport on May 5, 2012. In July 2012, he was sentenced to jail over a tweet that criticized the Bahraini prime minister.[17] Rajab and the other battle-hardened opposition activists knew that their struggle would not be won easily and were prepared to go to jail for their convictions. Rajab argued that the arrest of the opposition figure-heads broadened the social base of the movement and increased the number of supporters. For every arrested veteran, a dozen young activists emerged and would take their place. Sons, daughters, nephews, nieces, distant relatives, or just teenagers from the neighborhood would soon fill their places and become citizen journalists, human rights observers, and protest organizers. The best example of this would be the daughters of Abd al-Hadi al-Khawaja, Maryam and Zainab al-Khawaja, who became prominent activists in their own right. Their human rights activism inside and outside Bahrain played a significant role in getting international mainstream media coverage for Bahrain. After the arrest of her father, Maryam al-Khawaja became the vice-president of the Bahrain Center for Human Rights, and following the arrest of Nabil Rajab in 2012, Maryam became its acting president.[18] The fact that journalists and NGOs were often barred from entering Bahrain actually opened up spaces for these young activists and made them key in relating news about the protests to the outside world.

While these youth activists and the youth groups that emerged after February 14 were also attacked, their structures were less well known to the security services and they had only few visible figures who spoke out publicly. The 14 February Coalition, the main youth group that is driving the protests in Bahrain, has a central committee and branches in every Shia village and many urban quarters, but they operate underground. Many of its supporters were formerly followers of the unlicensed opposition groups Haqq and al-Wafa, but since their leaders have been jailed they support the Coalition. The 14 February Coalition has continued with weekly and sometimes

Human rights activists Nabil Rajab, second from right, and Zainab al-Khawaja, right, seen marching during clashes between pro-reform protesters and police in the old part of the Bahraini capital, Manama, on February 11, 2012. European Pressphoto Agency/Mazen Mahdi.

daily protests across the Shia villages, and at times also in Manama, which it documents in detail, and it is very effective at spreading news about the protests online.

Particularly after the crackdown in mid-March 2011, the 14 February Coalition became more confrontational, and its members started to use urban violence, such as the burning of tires, road-blocks, attacks on police stations, and skirmishes with security forces. With the political stalemate and repression ongoing, the

Coalition has become ever more popular and at least as important as al-Wifaq in Bahraini Shia politics. Some of the strongholds of the 14 February Coalition have seen the harshest security crackdowns and at times long sieges imposed on them by the security forces in retaliation for the actions of the Coalition. The Coalition has also established several sub-branches, including a military wing, the "Holy Defence" groups. The origins of these groups go back to a speech made by the Bahraini cleric Isa Qasim in January 2012, when he said that it was permissible to use violence to defend the community, and particularly the women of the Shia, after reports emerged that some women had been attacked. The ideology of the group is to defend what is considered holy to the Shia community, in other words, the women, the places of religious worship, and the properties of the community. Its supporters often wear headbands and T-shirts with the logo of the 14 February Coalition, cover their faces, and act as a kind of vigilante group in protests.[19]

The 14 February Coalition also tried to link its struggle with the global Occupy movement that emerged in 2011 and called for "Occupy Budaya" protests on Budaya Highway, a major traffic route that links several mainly Shia villages close to downtown Manama.[20]

At the middle of Budaya Highway lies a shopping center with a large Costa Coffee cafe that overlooks the highway. This particular coffee shop has become a popular hangout amongst opposition activists, particularly since the start of the crackdown in mid-March 2011. An apolitical Shia family owns the concession for Costa Coffee in Bahrain, while a Kuwaiti Sunni merchant family owns the Starbucks license for the Gulf states, and so pro-roundabout people and Bahraini Shia in general think they are somehow safer in a Costa Coffee shop than in a Starbucks.[21] When I sat there in May 2011, at the height of the repression campaign, one could often see a cascade of five or so trucks with macthine-guns mounted on top and armored personnel carriers coming from one

Police storm Budaya Highway in an attempt to regain control of it during clashes with protesters following the funeral procession of sixteen-year-old Ahmad Jabir al-Qatan in Abu Saiba village on the outskirts of the Bahraini capital, Manama, on October 7, 2011. European Pressphoto Agency/Mazen Mahdi.

side of the highway and crossing over to the other side. A few minutes later they would come back and then take the next exit. As my local interlocutors were arguing, these convoys were driving through the Shia villages that lined this major street—machine guns ready—simply to mark the presence of the security apparatus and perhaps arrest a few youths.

But even if protests occupy central places and highways, they will only constitute an existential threat to the monarchy if they are truly cross-sectarian and if the various Sunni constituencies of the regime start to turn against it. Of course, it is too easy to say that Shia went into the streets, and Sunnis stayed home. In fact in Bahrain, Sunnis had started to mobilize their own protests one week into the Pearl Roundabout protests in February 2011. Much of this was orchestrated and encouraged by the regime—pictures of the king and the prime minister were distributed at street corners, and many were largely responding to calls supporting the monarchy— but some protesters were more critical and voiced demands that were at times not dissimilar to those heard on the roundabout. Abdullatif al-Mahmud, who would later become the head of the first Sunni group to emerge out of the al-Fatih protests, the National Unity Gathering, initially demanded real concessions from the government and real political reforms. But the new Sunni political forces had limited independence vis-a-vis the power structures of the Al Khalifa.[22]

In May 2011, as I was hearing horrific stories about the crackdown from Shia human rights activists, Sunni politicians painted a different picture altogether. One day I was met at my hotel by a young Sunni who drove me to one of the main charities run by graduates of al-Azhar University in Cairo. From the beginning this young Sunni had been involved in organizing the pro-government protests at the al-Fatih mosque, through what later would become the al-Fatih Youth Union. He argued that he had done this because he did not see a place for himself at the roundabout, and because he was not happy with the radical slogans there. He and his friends wanted reforms, too, including more democracy, but they did not want a republic without the ruling family.

He was not afraid—this was his country and not much could happen to him. When we passed an army checkpoint with tanks that guarded the bridge between Manama and the largely Sunni island of Muharraq, he even suggested we get out and talk to the soldiers. He wanted to show me that this was the Bahraini and not the Saudi army, as had been suggested by the opposition. After the injuries I had seen over the past few months and the stories I had heard about the security forces I declined this invitation to chat with the soldiers. But the whole idea of stopping your car in front of an army checkpoint made up solely of Sunni soldiers and talking to them with a foreigner in your car would never have occurred to any of the Shia activists driving the protests on the ground, and was indicative as to how divided Bahrain had become.

In the huge salon of the Sunni charity (the Islamic Society), I met its elderly chairman, Abd al-Rahman Abd al-Salam, sitting in a corner on the sofa that lined all the walls of the salon. In terms of Bahraini politics he was high up, the head of a charity and a member of the royally appointed Consultative Council that the protesters on the Pearl Roundabout wanted dismantled.[23] The man I sat down with that evening struck me as a decent elderly man, engaged in charitable work and caring deeply about his community. But as soon as we started to talk about the Shia and the protest movement, his mood changed, and he made some of the grimmest statements I ever heard about the future of the Middle East. He used some of the most derogatory language to describe Shia Muslims. He called the Shia rejectionists as well as Zoroastrians, denouncing the Shia both as unbelievers and Persians. He applauded me for my endeavor to find out more about the Gulf Shia, since for him it was important to know more about the evil forces at work in the region. He argued that perhaps he would not see it, but, looking at me with his all-knowing stare, he proclaimed that I would certainly see the day when a fully fledged sectarian war would break out in the Gulf, and the Gulf Shia would take up arms at the bequest of their masters in Iran.

"It will take ten years at most until this happens, and Bahrain is their first target. After that they want to take over the Eastern Province. This is why we have to get at them now and show them that they will never succeed in this."

This was not a pretext to legitimize support for a dictatorial regime. He believed this would happen, and his conviction scared me.

Afterward, I went to a gathering of young Sunni activists organized by a senior member of the Muslim Brotherhood. Interestingly enough, the Bahraini Muslim Brotherhood is the only branch of the Brotherhood in the whole region that is pro-regime.[24] It is in quite a delicate situation, since several Gulf regimes started to see the Muslim Brotherhood as a severe threat to domestic security and regime stability, and in particular the UAE has cracked down on them. The Bahraini Muslim Brothers had a hard time explaining to me why they did not oppose the Al Khalifa, since monarchy does not fit into the political theory of the Muslim Brotherhood. They just argued that the Bahraini political system was different, and the ruling family not as bad as Assad or Mubarak.

It was here that I again met the young Sunni leftist woman I had spoken to on my first day at the Pearl Roundabout, who with her outspoken views had given such a powerful impression. I had not seen her for three months, and was surprised to see her here, at this gathering of pro-government Sunni youth activists and Muslim Brotherhood figures. But it soon became clear that she embodied the ways in which the sectarian counter-revolution had divided the country and changed the lives of all Bahrainis.

Soon after we had met she had fallen out with her friends. She had gone to the roundabout a couple of times but started criticizing the Shia slogans chanted by the Islamists. While the protesters' demands were not Shia per se, chants of "We want the fall of the regime" would often be followed by religious chants distinctive to

Shia Muslims, such as "With our soul, with our blood, we will defend you oh Hussayn," which rhymes with Bahrain.[25]

When she told her Shia secular friends that she did not like the Shia chants for Hussayn, that she could not relate to these slogans and that they would scare the Sunnis away, her Shia friends started to think of her as a traitor, as someone who could not be trusted. Some stopped answering their phones. And since she had joined the al-Fatih youth, she had hardly seen any Shia friends anymore. Like many other Sunnis that were initially in favor of the protest movement, she was eventually turned around into a regime supporter.

The reasons for this are neither solely the government-incited sectarian narrative nor the sectarian inclinations of parts of the protest movement. They are an interplay of top-down and bottom-up processes that divided the Bahraini protest movement along sectarian lines. But the arrival of Saudi troops, the ensuing crackdown, and the sectarianism of the regime's media hit the Shia exceptionally hard and made it socially acceptable to hate the other sect.

To appease its backers in the United States and Europe, the Bahraini ruling family undertook a number of "reconciliatory" steps after the crackdown in mid-March 2011. The Obama administration was especially embarrassed by the crackdown in Bahrain, as the whole world could see the hypocrisy of supporting democracy amongst foes but not amongst friends. In addition, the crackdown in Bahrain became increasingly used by Iran, Syria, and Russia to deflect attention from their own problems and the Syrian uprising. So the Bahraini rulers initiated the "National Dialogue" and established the Bahrain Independent Commission of Inquiry (BICI), which was to report to the king and was paid for by the king. The National Dialogue was held in July 2011, with the participation of some of the main legal opposition groups such as al-Wifaq and Wa'ad, but they soon withdrew after they realized they had been part of a public relations exercise and no results were to come from that dialogue.[26] The Bahraini opposition and the Shia at large also boycotted parliamentary by-elections held in September 2011 to replace the eighteen al-Wifaq MPs that had withdrawn from parliament at the start of the uprising.[27] There were several attempts to restart a dialogue, the last one in January 2013, in which Wa'ad and al-Wifaq participated, while the 14 February Coalition denounced the dialogue with the regime. But nothing indicated that this dialogue was not another public relations exercise to "buy time," and, so far, none of the dialogues have succeeded, as both sides remained deeply suspicious of each other, undermining the prospects of half-hearted negotiations.[28]

The BICI was established by royal decree on July 7 and began its investigative work later that month. It mainly looked into human rights violations by state agencies and, at the request of the government, by the protesters. Highly politicized in Bahrain and chaired by the Egyptian-American human rights lawyer Cherif Bassiouni, the commission carried out its work with fifty-one staff members and received over eight thousand complaints.

When the report was finally delivered to King Hamad on November 23, 2011, at a royal palace, everybody was surprised by the bluntness of the accusations against the Bahraini security forces.[29] The five-hundred-page report was a product of genuinely independent research and outlined authoritatively the human rights abuses, including systematic torture, committed by the security forces in February and March 2011. But it stopped short of the most sensitive issues. It did not incriminate those at the very top of the decision-making process, the senior members of the ruling family such as the king and the prime minister. It likewise refused to take a stance on whether Iran had stirred up the protests in Bahrain, or whether the GCC troops stationed in Bahrain had engaged in human rights abuses.[30]

The king and his Western backers could hitherto point to the fact that investigations were ongoing and that the recommendations of the BICI report were slowly being implemented. The regime came up with a report a year later arguing that Bahrain was on a reform path, that torture was uprooted, and that the recommendations were implemented.[31] Except that they were not, particularly not the more political recommendations such as the retrial of all those convicted in military or semi-military courts and under emergency law.[32] Unlike with other international commissions, which are usually administered by the UN, it was up to the king and an appointed implementation commission to decide which of the recommendations to implement and which not. Even Bassiouni himself was prompted to criticize the lack of implementation: "You can't say that justice has been done when calling for Bahrain to be a republic gets you a life sentence and the officer who repeatedly fired on an unarmed man at close range only gets seven years."[33] So instead of starting a process of transitional justice, the BICI has become a symbol of the political stalemate in Bahrain.

After the BICI report, two Western security officials with questionable track records were appointed to "reform" the Bahraini security forces. One of them, John Yates, had to resign from his position as assistant commissioner of the London Metropolitan Police because of the phone-hacking scandal by the Murdoch-owned British tabloid *News of the World*.[34] While these maneuvers were more directed at appeasing Bahrain's allies abroad, the crackdown at home continued unabated. To influence Western public opinion, the Bahraini regime has hired PR companies,[35] and it has also weaponized less visible and lethal means of coercion. It has mainly relied on an extensive use of tear gas against protesters, including in confined spaces, which has led to several dozen casualties since 2011.[36]

As if there had not been enough structural violence, the regime tried everything to destroy the memory of the uprising. Four days after the entry of Saudi troops, on March 18, 2011, the Pearl Monument was torn down. Thereby the image of the Pearl Monument became an even more powerful icon of resistance, one that is sprayed in graffiti all over the walls of Bahrain. It has also become the icon of choice for opposition supporters on social media, has been rebuilt in all kinds of shapes and forms, and has even become the logo of an opposition satellite TV channel based in London.[37]

To make clear that this was a victory of the Sunnis over the Shia, the junction that was built to replace the Pearl Roundabout was called Faruq Junction in honor of caliph Umar ibn al-Khattab. Umar was the second caliph of Islam, who is revered by Sunnis as a great military leader. He conquered large parts of the Eastern Roman Empire and the Iranian Sassanid Empire, but Shia generally do not accept the first three caliphs as righteous successors of Muhammad and dislike Umar. By tearing down the Pearl Monument then, the regime turned a symbol of national heritage, of Gulf unity, and of hope for a more democratic future into a symbol of sectarianism. The traffic intersection that was the Pearl Roundabout has been heavily guarded by tanks and special forces ever since so as to prevent protestors from returning.

5 A SAUDI ACHILLES HEEL

"We are not loyal to other countries or authorities, nor are we loyal to this country. What is this country? The regime that oppresses me? The regime that steals my money, sheds my blood, and violates my honor? What does a country mean? The regime? The Ruling clan? The soil? I don't know what a country means. Loyalty is only to Allah! We have declared, and we reiterate, that our loyalty is to Allah, not the Saud clan."

—*Nimr al-Nimr, Awwamiyya, Eastern Province, October 7, 2011*[1]

"Their behavior constitutes a new sort of terrorism led by a minority. . . . Security men in the Kingdom of Saudi Arabia will deal resolutely and with an iron fist with such cases. . . . This minority was lured by foreign hands unpleased of the Kingdom of Saudi Arabia's honorable positions towards the Arab and Islamic nation. . . . They use such ignorant and young men as a fifth column that achieves their plots and alleviate the pressure mounted on them."

—*Official Saudi security source, quoted by Saudi Press Agency, February 20, 2012*[2]

Since 2011, Saudi Arabia has seen the largest street protests the country has ever known. Most dissent came from Shia Muslims in the Eastern Province, but there were small protests, petitions, and criticisms of the ruling family in various other parts of the kingdom. The repression of protests led to the death of at least fifteen Shia youths. Western media and the Arab media controlled by Gulf rulers have stayed largely silent, partly because the Saudi government prevents journalists and researchers from traveling to the Shia areas of the Eastern Province. When large-scale protests started in Bahrain on February 14, 2011, in the space of one day the GCC regimes lost their aura of being immune to demands for democratic change. Those who live closest to Bahrain, just a thirty-minute drive across the causeway, were amongst the first to be inspired. The sectarian discrimination that Saudi Shia endure, which effectively makes them second-class citizens, made them more prone to protest against the government.

Anti-Shiism remains very common in government and amongst many Saudis. This is partly due to textbooks used in schools, in which Shia and other sects and religions are decried as unbelievers, as those that reject the oneness of God (*tawhid*). The Saudi rivalry with Iran and particularly the sectarian response to the Arab Spring have exacerbated these views, making it ever more acceptable to voice derogatory remarks against Shia in public. There has never been a Shia minister, and Shia are largely barred from the foreign and security services, the military, the police, as well as sensitive positions in the oil and other key industries. They face persecution by the religious police for their religious rituals, and their mosques and prayer houses often operate in a sort of legal gray area and can be closed anytime.

Since 2003, Saudi Shia leaders have been invited to take part in the National Dialogue, initiated by Crown Prince and later King Abdullah. This was a key part of the attempt by Abdullah to present himself as the "reformist" king who would initiate political changes in the country. The National Dialogue was a series of discussions

Opposition cleric Nimr al-Nimr at a protest in Awwamiyya, Saudi Arabia, on February 10, 2012. Photo by a local photographer who wishes to remain anonymous.

across the country involving representatives from many different Saudi constituencies, including conservative clerics, liberals, religious minorities, and women. He introduced elections for half the seats in largely powerless municipal councils. In 2005, when Saudi Arabia held its first municipal elections since the 1960s, Shia turned out in great numbers in the Eastern Province, electing many Shia to municipal councils in Qatif and al-Ahsa because they saw this as a sign to mark their presence. To some degree, the government has begun to allow the observance of Shia holidays such as Ashura in majority-Shia areas. But in practice, discrimination in government jobs and schools continues, and anti-Shia sentiments thrive.[3] The overall assessment of King Abdullah's reign is meager.[4]

When I first visited Saudi Arabia in late 2008, years before the Arab Spring, I felt dissatisfaction among Saudi Shia youths with the National Dialogue, the powers of the municipal councils, the lack of political reform, and the continuing arrests and harassment by the religious police. Some even argued that the youths could not be appeased anymore. I vividly remember a late-night drive from Qatif down dusty streets lined with thousands of date palms to one of the outlying villages. The man I was about to meet had been a local leader of the rebellion in the Eastern Province in 1979, as were hundreds of others of his generation; had led a cell in his village; and after the uprising had fled into exile, first to Iran and then to the Shia Shrine city of Sayyida Zeinab outside of Damascus. Contrary to the *shirazi* leaders such as cleric Hasan al-Saffar, the spiritual leader of the Saudi *shirazi* movement, many local *shirazi* leaders who stayed in Saudi Arabia, and some of the clerics abroad, were critical of doing a deal with the government that would not include major changes in the situation of the Saudi Shia. But when a deal was struck in 1993 they eventually came home and tried to work within the system. However, those critical of the deal remained so, and started to criticize both the government and what they saw as a class of "new notables" formed of co-opted former opposition activists.[5]

The flashing lights of an oil-drilling pump that stood just a few yards away illuminated the road leading up to the house of the cleric. And when we got out of the car I could hear its noise vividly: tak tak tak tak. I was told the drilling hardly stopped, day or night. We entered through the back of a small garden to the *majlis* of the cleric. A *majlis* is often quite a large communal space where people come together in someone's house to discuss and socialize. But his *majlis* was not as grand as the ones I had seen in Riyadh, Jeddah, or even Qatif;[6] it was a small basement room crammed with books and a few mats on the floor, where he said he was teaching pupils most days to make up for the lack of proper Shia religious schools in Saudi Arabia.

We sat down on the floor, and he made us tea. And then he spoke out against the ruling family, and against the co-opted *shirazis*, and argued that a new movement should be formed, that the current approach had not achieved its aims. "As you see, we live on top of the oil, I see how it is being taken out of our soil every day. But you also see that our areas are poor, and we do not get a fair share of the oil income, much of it is wasted through corruption in the ruling family."

I felt a bit awkward; here I was, at the heart of Western security interests in the region, on top of the largest oil reserves in the world, in one of the most securitized states in the world, and a long-time opposition cleric was telling me how they were changing tactics and wanted to start working against the government again. I asked myself if the state and its foreign allies—particularly the United States—were aware of these tensions, and why they were not trying to address some of the underlying problems. After all, these people had decades of experience in oppositional politics, they had networks in every village, and several million people were deeply frustrated with the way they were being treated. Would it not be smart to appease them in some way or another? But serious appeasement of the Shia was not on the agenda. Supporters of the regime often countered that the *Wahhabi* clergy would block any substantial change in the position of the Shia.

Protesters pass the "Pearl Roundabout of Qatif," a roundabout outside of Qatif, Saudi Arabia, that was nicknamed in reference to the Pearl Roundabout in Bahrain, after opposition cleric Nimr al-Nimr was arrested on July 8, 2012. Photo by a local photographer who wishes to remain anonymous.

Three months after this meeting, in February 2009, clashes broke out at the al-Baqi' cemetery in Medina between Eastern Province Shia and Sunnis as well as security forces, leading to follow-up demonstrations in the Eastern Province. Observing the protests in 2009 as well as those since 2011, I had to think of what the cleric had told me that night in 2008: "There is a new youth movement that can not be controlled anymore and does not listen to their fathers. And there is a group of *shirazis* that does not want to go along with the pro-government path of the Shia leadership."

One of those clerics, Nimr al-Nimr from Awwamiyya, was the only local cleric to openly endorse the protests in the Eastern Province from February 17, 2011 onward, and he became something of a figurehead for the young protesters. Awwamiyya has long been a hotspot of oppositional Shia political movements. It was here in 2009 that al-Nimr said that Shia might one day seek the secession of the Eastern Province and hundreds took to the streets to protest the regime's treatment of the Shia. This statement from al-Nimr, a long-time opposition figure who renounced any engagement with the state, seemed to confirm the worst fears of the Saudi ruling family about the loyalty of Saudi Shia and broke a taboo.[7] Many had been arrested in the aftermath of the 2009 protests, and two years later the February 17 protesters demanded the release of three activists that remained in jail. The regime, wary that the situation might escalate, released the three and a number of other Shia prisoners. For a couple of days, it seemed as if an uneasy calm had returned to the Eastern Province. But as the protests in Bahrain intensified, protesters in the Eastern Province returned to the streets. Their next demand was for the release of nine Shia prisoners imprisoned for their alleged involvement in the Khobar Towers bombings of 1996, which killed nineteen American servicemen. The nine had been indicted in the United States in 2001 and were accused of conspiring with Lebanese Hizbullah and Iran. But as American foreign policy priorities changed after 9/11 they became the "forgotten prisoners," the name they came to be known by amongst Saudi Shia.[8] Their pictures were held up at rallies that demanded their release.

Though relatively small, protests over the following weeks grew to a few hundred participants, particularly on Thursdays and Fridays, and mainly in Awwamiyya and Qatif. But after the planned Day of Rage across Saudi Arabia failed to spill over to other regions on March 11, 2011, the Saudi regime regained its confidence, repressing dissent at home and vying for influence in the countries whose leaders had fallen, trying to protect its interests against those of other regional powers. The Saudi media, alongside the media and regimes of the other GCC member states, portrayed the uprisings in Bahrain and the protests in the Eastern Province as carried out by Iranian agents, casting doubt on the loyalty of their Shia citizens. This discourse had been used over and over since the Iranian Revolution in 1979. After Abdullah became king in 2005, it should have been replaced by one of national dialogue and co-existence, but by 2011 the narrative of the Shia fifth column was back on the front pages of Saudi newspapers. It is a dangerous game used by the Saudi regime to scare the majority of the population into trusting the ruling family as the sole guarantor of stability.

While small protests continued for two months in the Eastern Province, they lost momentum after the crackdown on the protest movement in Bahrain and after it had become clear that the rest of the country would not join in. Although there was online campaigning for the release of Khalid al-Juhani, the lone protester who turned up to the protests on March 11 in Riyadh, protests remained limited. Another blow to the demonstrations in the Eastern Province came in the form of a statement on April 21 calling for a halt of protests, signed by thirty-five Saudi Shia clerics, including Hasan al-Saffar. The Saudi state did not make any concessions and arrested over a hundred protesters, thereby laying the grounds for a much larger protest campaign in the fall.

Within a few months, the achievements of the National Dialogue, which had led to an awareness of and a certain respect for diversity within Saudi Arabia, were destroyed and replaced by big-otry and sectarian hatred. When a skirmish occurred outside a police station in the village of Awwamiyya on October 2, this was wholeheartedly blamed on agents of a foreign power, a not-so-veiled reference to Iran, and cartoons and editorials in Saudi newspapers presented the Shia as disloyal traitors. This event indeed was a significant development, but Shia activists tell a very different story. They relate that the authorities arrested the fathers of two young activists who had been sought for the protests in March in order to force the youths to hand themselves in. As news of the arrests spread throughout the village, villagers began to pro-test in front of the police station. The police fired into the air to disperse the crowd, unaware that some of the protesters had brought their own firearms with them. The videos posted online do not allow a decision about who fired first, but both sides were armed and this eventually led to a night of actual guerrilla warfare around the police station and in later hours in side streets and the outskirts of Awwamiyya. In total, about a dozen policemen were injured.[9]

After these events, the security forces cordoned off the Shia areas and set up checkpoints in Qatif and the surrounding vil-lages. On November 20, one Shia teenager, Nasir al-Muhayshi, was shot dead in Qatif. Shia activists claim that he was walking in the streets when he was shot and that his body was not released, which led to a protest the next day. During this protest, another protester, Ali al-Filfil, was killed, and the feelings amongst the citi-zens were running high. The government claims that the security forces were shot at by "aggressors," and in the resulting exchanges of gunfire at checkpoints two civilians died.[10] While this narrative might have convinced some in Riyadh, Qatif was on fire. On November 23, tens of thousands took to the streets of Qatif for the funeral of the two fallen youths. A dangerous spiral of protest, repression, and public funerals had been set in motion, which had catalyzed much of the Arab Spring protests. Funerals were key in the Arab Spring, since they drew large crowds and emotions were already high because of the deaths. In many cases, confrontational tactics by the security forces heightened these tensions and led to further clashes and casualties. The first days of the uprising in Bahrain, for example, saw several mass funerals that turned into political protests. Across Syria, funerals were key in mobilizing all segments of society, and in deepening disdain of the regime in rural areas, villages, and popular urban quarters.

In the Qatif demonstration on November 23, protesters chanted "Death to Al Saud" along with other slogans that called for the downfall of the governor of the Eastern Province, Prince Muhammad bin Fahd. These chants crossed a line, directly attacking the ruling family. The response was swift: two more protesters were killed on that day, "due to the exchange of gunfire with unknown criminal elements who have infiltrated among citizens" as the Saudi Ministry of Interior put it.[11]

I arrived in Riyadh in late November at the height of these events and on the eve of the month of Muharram, on the tenth day of which Shia Muslims mourn the battle of Karbala and the death of Imam Hussayn, the grandson of the Prophet Muhammad. Against all odds it rained heavily when I touched down in Riyadh, and the streets were flooded. Saudi Arabia was unprepared for heavy rains, and therefore the government had decided to turn the day into a school holiday, a move that led to a series of cynical comments on social media networks. Heavy rains in Jeddah had caused floods in 2009 and early 2011, with more than a hundred casualties. A corruption scam was uncovered, and it turned out that planned-and-paid-for structures to deal with floods had never been built. The rage of Jeddah residents and several small protests this year were probably as worrisome to the Saudi regime as the protests in the East, and the upper echelon of the ruling family was quick to try to prove to the citizenry that it was dealing with this form of bad government in an effective way. Governors and ministers were portrayed in the Saudi media

Protesters carrying Bahraini flags demand the fall of the governor of the Eastern Province, Muhammad bin Fahd, in Qatif, Saudi Arabia, on January 6, 2012. Photo by a local photographer who wishes to remain anonymous.

touring the flood-affected areas, promising investigations, new projects, and more "development".[12]

"The state has a plan to deal with Shia grievances through development," a senior official of the Ministry of Interior in Riyadh said. "But we can't give the Shia special rights just because of their sectarian affiliation, or we would have to do this for other groups as well." This narrative has been in place for decades, at least since the underdevelopment of Shia regions was recognized by the state following the uprising in 1979. But this strategy is not implemented fully. While I was prevented from going to Qatif during this visit—"for my own safety"—I had visited Qatif and the surrounding villages in 2008. Many of these areas have the feeling of slums, with mud roads, decaying old city centers, and uncontrolled new property developments at their outskirts. Officials in Riyadh maintain that there are other regions that are similarly poor and have not much political say, such as areas in the north and the south of the country.

Reinforced by the official portrayal of this year's events, opinions about the Shia in Riyadh reached the point of racist derogatory stereotyping. I had an honest discussion about the situation of Shia in Saudi Arabia with an academic at a major research center in Riyadh, when he advised me to pay particular attention to their religious rituals. I said that they are very similar to the rituals of Shia communities in other countries. But he looked at me with an all-knowing stare and replied, "Tomorrow is Ashura and you know what they do then?" Without waiting for my response he insisted, "At midnight they switch off the light and have group sex! They don't care whose wife it is, and then the women bear the children of random men." With these absurd views prevailing amongst some Sunnis, it is no wonder that many Shia do not feel at home in the Saudi polity, and are even thinking of emigrating.

A full-scale uprising during Ashura arguably was prevented only by a statement issued by clerics from all the major Shia political trends that urged their followers not to employ violence against the security forces and not to use the holiday for political statements.

The signatories were the leading clerics of the two strands of political Islam amongst Saudi Shia, the *shirazi* and the local Saudi Hizbullah networks, as well as of the traditionalist notable families. The latter had been the main intermediaries with the state until the former opposition groups, mainly the *shirazis*, had made a deal with King Fahd in 1993.

These leaders, who came of age during the period of Islamist grass-roots mobilization in the Eastern Province in the late 1970s and 1980s, are being challenged by a younger generation, which does not necessarily believe in the old conflicts that divided the Shia political groups. As elsewhere in the Arab world, they are media-savvy and disenfranchised from their political elite, be they notables or former opposition activists, and they want to capitalize on the Arab uprisings around them.

The ruling family had had an opportunity after the small protests in March to instigate some democratic reforms, or at least make major concessions toward its Shia citizens that would have given them some say in the country's politics and made them feel part of the Saudi polity. Instead, the regime opted for repression over the summer months, arresting those involved in the March protests. But the Arab Spring has fundamentally altered the equation and given hope to Saudi citizens; the old tactics of repression, defamation, and media blackout have not worked anywhere else in the Arab world and are unlikely to work indefinitely in Saudi Arabia. Resentment against the unequal distribution of wealth runs high all over the country, not just in the Eastern Province. In other parts of Saudi, the protest campaigns have mainly been for the release of political prisoners, such as those accused of having links to al-Qaeda. While these are generally small flash-mob-like protests with a few dozen participants, they have occurred in areas that are key power bases of the Saudi regime such as Riyadh, Buraida, and Dammam.[13] Buraida, the capital of al-Qasim province, lies in the historical heartland of the *Wahhabiyya* and of dissident Islamist movements, including al-Qaeda, and so Buraida has a high percentage of political prisoners. Because of its centrality to the Saudi system, the protests for the release of prisoners in Buraida, which often include women, are particularly worrying to the regime. The arrest of eleven women at a protest in the city of Buraida on January 5, 2013, for the release of political prisoners was caught on video.[14] In early March 2013, a number of women and men even camped out in Buraida, trying to establish a protest square, and the next morning 161 of them were arrested.[15]

A group of reformers mainly from Jeddah and Riyadh have tried to establish the first political parties and independent human rights organizations in the country. They have become more out-spoken since the start of the Arab Spring, but retribution was swift. The leaders of the Saudi Civil and Political Rights Associa-tion, which has detailed human rights violations and unfair trials against political dissidents, have been convicted and sentenced to ten and eleven years in prison.[16] There has also been an upsurge in women's activism since 2011. Female university students have pro-tested repeatedly across the country, starting in Abha. Women's activists have also intensified their campaign to gain the right to drive.[17]

King Abdullah actually made some concessions to Saudi women, even though their political importance should not be exagger-ated. He named thirty women to the Majlis al-Shura council, the appointed advisory council with no legislative powers, in January 2013, and he promised women the right to vote and run for office in municipal elections in 2015.[18] Promptly, however, a group of clerics demonstrated outside the royal court against the appointment of women and demanded to meet the king and his royal court chief of staff to give them advice. Thereby, they defied both the official clergy, who had forbidden such demonstrations, and the Saudi rul-ers.[19] Sunni Islamists have become increasingly more vocal. Salman al-Awda, a former leader of the *Sahwa*, the Saudi Islamist opposi-tion movement that emerged after the 1990–91 Gulf War, and one of the foremost Sunni Islamist critics of the Saudi government, had signed a petition in March 2011 calling for a constitutional monarchy, and reiterated his calls in a highly publicized open letter to the government on March 15, 2013. In the letter he warned of a socio-political explosion if political prisoners were not released and reforms were not enacted immediately.[20]

Many of the more peripheral regions of Saudi Arabia are poor and lack the lifestyle associated with the wealthy Saudis of Riyadh and Jeddah. This is true for the northern and southern regions of the country. But the problem is that in the Eastern Province, political economy and regional discrimination overlap with sect, and this is no coincidence. In December 2011 I took a train from the capital Riyadh to Hofuf in the Eastern al-Ahsa oasis, which is made up more or less equally of Sunni and Shia. The railroad had been built by the Americans to connect the oil industry in the east to the capital. The next day I had lunch with a Shia lawyer, whom I had met in 2008. He came to the lobby of my hotel, where I wanted to hold our meeting. Anxiously, he sat down, hesitant to speak. I asked him if something was wrong, perhaps with the hotel. No, he said, "This is a hotel owned by a Shia family." I had not known this but it explained why the television in my room had all the Shia satellite television stations streaming in from Kuwait, Iraq, Lebanon, and Iran. In fact, I could now understand how, in this virtual world, I could see some of the prominent clerics from Qatif such as Hasan al-Saffar, Munir al-Khabbaz, or Fawzi al-Sayf on television in Saudi Arabia even though no Shia satellite channel is allowed to broadcast from Saudi Arabia. Their sermons in Qatif are recorded and streamed directly to the channels in Kuwait that beam them back into the Eastern Province, where people that cannot attend a particular *hussainiyya* or mosque can see them. There is hardly a better way to describe how mass media can forge collective identities amongst a people the state is desperately trying to keep divided. So even though I was prevented from going to Qatif—"for my own safety," I could sit a 140 kilometers away in Hofuf and watch the sermons in real time. And while the sermons did not address the recent protests outright, they used the language of oppression and resistance that is key to the discourse of Ashura, and everyone knew that the clerics were talking about the repressive actions of the state, in Saudi Arabia, Bahrain and beyond.

In the lobby of the hotel, my friend pointed to a man sitting behind us, indicating he was a security agent. I was not particularly surprised, given the tensions in the country, and also did not have any illusions that we could shake them off, but I got into the car with my friend anyway, and we went to a restaurant in a different part of town. His windshield was still splintered in the same way as it had been three years ago, broken from a stone that hit it on one of the mud roads in the Shia villages of al-Ahsa. Over lunch he told me how he and his fellow activists believed in the success of the Arab uprisings, even in Saudi Arabia and even if it would take a long time: "The Arab train against the repressive regimes has departed, there is no turning it back. We have promised our children that they will grow up in dignity, not the way we had to grow up."

He argued that after initial protests in the spring, the government arrested many protesters, but community leaders had agreed that it was best to stop protests and negotiate with the government, as the Shia were too weak to protest alone. Over the summer they were hoping for some response from the government, and some concessions, but this hope was in vain. The Shia activists could not even mobilize people for the municipal elections held in September 2011. The elections were supposed to be held in 2009 but were delayed, and the announcement that they would be held in 2011 was the first political "concession" made by the Saudi king, Abdullah, after the start of the Arab Spring. The limited participation in the elections across the country indicated a general disenfranchisement with institutionalized politics and the limited powers of the municipal councils.[21]

Reading through the newspapers back in Riyadh I was baffled that the Shia issue and the protests in the Eastern Province had made it to the front pages of Saudi newspapers. The protests in spring had not been discussed in Saudi media; discussions there were confined to threatening statements by the Interior Ministry and official religious scholars. But now, since the shooting in Awwamiyya in October 2011 and particularly the mass protests in late November, the regime felt that the Shia protests were best publicly discussed and labeled as an Iranian conspiracy. It also forced all the Shia notables and clerical leaders to come forward and publicly, in the press, apologize for the bad behavior of some of the Shia youth, as those who did not would be labeled as the worst of traitors. Statements by the Ministry of Interior referred to "instigators of sedition, discord and unrest that were acting at the behest of a foreign country seeking to undermine the security and stability of the homeland,"[22] a not-so-thinly veiled reference to Iran. Though the narrative of the Shia as Iranian agents had been used immediately after the Iranian Revolution, there had been almost no direct allegations of that nature in the official Saudi media since the late 1990s, particularly not since the start of the National Dialogue. But here was the Ministry of Interior saying just that. The statement and pictures of hooded youths burning tires and driving motorbikes spread within a few hours in Saudi media. After Muharram 2011 passed without major demonstrations, the state started a fresh arrest campaign, offering financial rewards for information leading to the arrest of twenty-three Shia youths, initiating an actual manhunt in the Eastern Province and further inflaming the situation.[23]

Feelings amongst Saudi Shia again ran high before the one-year anniversary of the uprising in Bahrain on February 14, 2012. On Thursday February 9, a celebration in Qatif of the birthday of the Prophet Muhammad, which Shia commemorate but Sunnis do not, turned into a demonstration calling for reforms and the release of prisoners, after which the protester Munir al-Maydani was shot dead. A day later, after Friday prayers, another protester, Zuhayr Al Said, was killed. Their funeral procession again turned into huge

demonstrations on February 13 in Qatif and Awwamiyya, with tens
of thousands of participants.

When I spoke to some of my Saudi Shia friends on the phone,
they were appalled by the government's reaction, but also said that
they personally had very limited powers to stop the youths from
protesting. One story I was told was of a father who tried to prevent his son from going to the nightly protests in Qatif. The father
had been a member of the Shia opposition in the 1980s and had
lived abroad in exile, where his son was born. He returned in 1993
and stopped his oppositional and political activities. When the
Arab Spring swept across the region, his son, now in his early
twenties, became active online and soon went out to the demonstrations. One evening, a day after a young Shia had been shot
dead by the security forces and feelings were running high, his
father tried to talk him out of it and closed the door in front of his
son. He told his son that he should not go out, that he feared for
his son's life. He argued that it would not lead to anything, and
that when he and his own friends were young they had, for over a
decade, tried to fight against this regime, but to no avail. There
was no other option than to sit and wait, and hope that some
gains could be secured through dialogue. Furious, the son replied,
"You destroyed the livelihood of the family, we had to grow up in
exile in Syria, and when we came back to Saudi we did not have
anything, we had to start from scratch. We were poorer than our
neighbors because you went away. If it was not for your convictions, then why did you do it? You have lost our family's wealth,
and you sold out your beliefs by coming back home. And now
you want to prevent me from fighting for my convictions?"

The son had won the argument, and the father let him out into
the night of Qatif to protest in the face of the security forces, just
as he had done three decades earlier in 1979, when he had seen
some of his friends shot dead.

But after these last killings, even Hasan al-Saffar, who had been
the main intermediary between the Shia community and the

Protesters raise a banner declaring "Here is the Republic of al-Ahsa and Qatif: Not the Kingdom of Wahhabism and Al Saud" and bearing the name of the Coalition for Freedom and Justice in Qatif, Saudi Arabia, on July 10, 2012. Photo by a local photographer who wishes to remain anonymous.

government for two decades, and had been repeatedly received by King Abdullah, spoke out. While he had previously urged protesters to remain at home, he now criticized the security forces for killing young Shia. The response was swift: the Interior Ministry attacked him harshly, denouncing the protests in Qatif as the "new terrorism" that would be handled "with an iron fist."[24]

The Eastern Province was relatively calm for several months until the arrest of Nimr al-Nimr on July 8 started a third protest cycle.[25] His arrest gave the Shia youth another cause that brought thousands to the streets. Immediately after his arrest, large demonstrations erupted in Qatif and two protesters were shot dead, Akbar al-Shakhuri from Awwamiyya and Muhammad al-Filfil from Shuwaikha.[26] Young activists started to adopt the tactics of the Bahraini youth, including the use of Molotov cocktails against government buildings and police patrols and the nightly burning of tires on roads. Some youth and opposition groups formed a decentralized coalition, the Coalition for Freedom and Justice.[27] The security forces, meanwhile, continued to hunt those on a list of twenty-three wanted, and in their raids in late September killed or injured several of them.[28] On December 27, 2012, eighteen-year-old Ahmad Al Matar was shot dead by the security forces, and his funeral turned into a large demonstration.[29]

While the replacement in January 2013 of Muhammad bin Fahd, the long-serving governor of the Eastern Province, with Saud bin Nayef gave the Shia some hope of a fresh start, repression against government critics and anti-Shia incitement have not subsided since.[30] The regime moved ahead with trials against those arrested for political subversion, both Sunni and Shia. In March 2013, the public prosecutor even demanded the death penalty, possibly by crucifiction, for the cleric Nimr al-Nimr, causing outrage amongst the Shia. At the same time, sixteen Saudi Shia, one Lebanese, and one Iranian were arrested in cities throughout the kingdom, including in Mecca, Riyadh, and the Eastern Province, and accused of having formed a spy cell at the behest of Iran. Saudi media again portrayed all Saudi Shia as disloyal.[31] Saudi

Shia notables from Qatif and al-Ahsa, including Hasan al-Saffar, signed several statements that refuted the allegations and the targeting of the Shia community as a whole. Thereafter, most of the signatories, including senior leaders of the *shirazis*, were questioned by the security forces, and many were banned from traveling abroad.[32]

So, while the Saudi ruling family, through its use of handouts of wealth, repression, and sectarianism, managed to survive the Arab Spring and prevent mass protests by Shia and Sunnis around a common cause, this led to a severe worsening of the relationship between the Saudi Shia and the state, to the extent that distrust between the two sides has probably never been as high since the Iranian revolution in 1979. Because the root causes of the protests in the Eastern Province have not been addressed, there likely will be more protests in the future, as well as more violence from the state. And while the state relentlessly used the "Shia threat" narrative to scare the Sunnis, there were signs that protests for the release of political prisoners and demands for political reform were no longer confined to the Eastern Province, but were spreading to Buraida and Riyadh in the heartland of the Saudi state.

6 THE ORANGE MOVEMENT

"We will not allow you, your highness, to take Kuwait into the abyss of autocracy. . . . We no longer fear your prisons and your baton sticks."

—Musallam al-Barrak, October 15, 2012,
Irada Square, Kuwait City[1]

"We will not condone street chaos, riot or any action that stymies public life and work. We will not allow seeds of seditions to be grown in our dear country. We will not allow violence and chaos to spread among our youth. We will not let anybody mislead our dear youth with illusions and lies. We will not allow the hijacking of the nation's will through empty calls and false heroism."

—Sabah al-Ahmad al-Jabir al-Sabah, Amir of Kuwait,
October 19, 2012, Kuwait City[2]

Kuwait, too, experienced youth-led mass protests in the wake of the Arab Spring, with the largest political demonstrations to date from October to December 2012. The popularity of the youth movement became clear to me when I attended a dinner party of the Kuwaiti young and fashionable in December 2012. My host had invited me to give me a break from work, from talking about politics, but at the party of well-off twenty- and thirtysomethings all the talk was about the recent political events in the country. Economically, these people could not complain. They were the sons and daughters of the old merchant families who had engaged in long-distance trade, pearling, and after the discovery of oil grew ever richer by securing government contracts and monopolizing certain sectors of the economy. Many of these young people already headed companies or branches of their parents' business conglomerates. Their parents' generation had in the 1950s and 1960s been inspired by Arab nationalism and leftist ideologies, and had sought to curtail the power of the ruling family via nationalist rhetoric. To counter these Arab nationalist merchant families, the Kuwaiti ruling family formed new alliances and encouraged the immigration and naturalization of tribal groups that settled at the periphery of Kuwait city. This exacerbated the division between the long sedentarized groups, the *hadar*, and the Bedouins, the *badu*.[3]

But to my surprise, many at the party supported the protest movement and some had even been tear-gassed at the protests themselves. Perhaps the strongest advocate of the protest movement was also the most unlikely. A gay architect in his early thirties, he spent much of his time in Europe and traveling the region to supervise his projects. There was not much that he personally had in common with some of the leaders of the Kuwaiti opposition, which includes *salafis*, tribal figures, and septuagenarian leftists. But he said he fully supported the protest movement and had seldom felt so empowered as when he attended one of the large protests with tens of thousands of participants in November. Another descendant from one of the wealthiest merchant families whom I met separately explained to me that he had initially been skeptical of the protests and went along with some friends to the first large protest on October 15 merely out of curiosity. These protests came to be known as Dignity of a Nation (*Karamat Watan*), named after the anonymous Twitter account that was calling for protests and directed them around town.[4] The October 15 protest was attacked by security forces, who teargassed protesters, beat them with batons, and arrested some. This repression, which for Kuwaiti standards was severe and unheard of in recent years, radicalized him. This was the day he decided to put his efforts into changing the political system of the country, as he felt a deep sense of belonging, perhaps for the first time ever, to the country and its citizens. He said that when running from the tear gas it did not matter that many of the other people at the protest had long beards, the hallmark of the *salafis*, and that many came from tribes that lived in less-well-off areas and with whom he might never have interacted beforehand. The support for the protest movement then came from a whole range of sectors of Kuwaiti society, from all classes, sects, and tribes, and so as in Bahrain and Saudi Arabia the ruling family and its allies had to come up with a narrative that divided the protesters and prevented a possible common opposition front. This narrative was the *badu-hadar* divide.

So while there are similarities, for example in the divide-and-rule strategies of the government and in the demands of the opposition for a constitutional monarchy, the Kuwaiti case is quite distinct from those of Bahrain and Saudi Arabia. But the sectarian fallout from the protests in Bahrain and Saudi Arabia profoundly affected Kuwaiti politics and society, making it a key arena of the sectarian Gulf.

I had also visited Kuwait in late February 2012, after Prime Minister Nasser al-Muhammad al-Sabah had been ousted and a new majority opposition parliament had been elected. It had already become clear that the dreams of the Arab Spring would take longer than a few months to materialize, and Syria had descended into civil war. Kuwait has a population between 2.5 and 3 million people, of whom 1.3 million are Kuwaiti citizens. Between 20 and 30 percent of Kuwaiti citizens are Shia, and they hail originally from

Iran, Iraq, Saudi Arabia (al-Ahsa), and Bahrain, with the biggest group (70 percent of the Shia) being of Iranian origin.[5] They often retain a strong group identity and links to their places of origin.[6] Many Kuwaiti Shia as well as Sunni liberals had viewed the protests in Bahrain with enthusiasm and were appalled by the government crackdown there. Some Shia started to mobilize in support of Bahrain and staged small demonstrations in Kuwait.[7] Reflecting the delicate sectarian balance in Kuwait and the prominence of the Shia notable families, the Kuwaiti amir Sabah al-Ahmad al-Jabir al-Sabah personally tried to mediate between the Bahraini opposition and the ruling family at several points in February and March 2011. But his efforts were sharply rebuked by the Bahraini ruling family.[8] As a result, Kuwait stayed largely out of the crackdown in Bahrain, as some Shia Kuwaiti soldiers reportedly refused to participate in the GCC intervention in Bahrain as part of the Peninsula Shield Force.[9] As a compromise, Kuwait sent a symbolic detachment of naval units that could not be used against Bahraini protesters.[10]

Many Sunni Islamists in Kuwait, on the other hand, lauded the government crackdown on protesters in Bahrain. With the start of the mass protests in Syria, and the heavy involvement of Sunni Islamists there, these Sunnis also started to mobilize support for the Syrian opposition and demanded that Kuwait supply them with arms.[11] In February 2012, most Shia I spoke to were deeply suspicious of the intentions of the new parliament. Sunni Islamists, particularly the *salafis* and the Muslim Brotherhood, and tribal figures had mobilized by resorting to identity politics, a populist rhetoric that was often based on communal, sectarian, or tribal identities, and had won a landslide victory in the parliamentary elections held on February 2, 2012.[12] Four MPs came from the Kuwaiti branch of the Muslim Brotherhood, making it for a brief period the most powerful and visible branch of the Muslim Brotherhood in the Gulf states.[13] In total, thirty-five MPs in the parliament sought to curtail the authoritarianism of the ruling family and formed a so-called "majority bloc," seeking greater accountability, more democracy, and an investigation of corruption allegations. This was arguably the first time a staunch majority of parliament was against the ruling family, and the ruling family saw the "majority bloc" as a foremost political threat.

One evening in February 2012 I did what most male Kuwaitis of a certain age do: I went to a number of *diwaniyyas*, or discussion gatherings, that are held in *Diwans*, salons attached to houses or in the case of the wealthiest men large buildings, to sip tea and talk politics. One *diwaniyya* I went to was hosted by a well-known Shia journalist and included a prominent group of mainly Shia intellectuals, journalists, and politicians. They explained to me how Kuwait had become a regional hub for religious television channels and other media and how its media sector had became embroiled in the sectarian Gulf. Because of its relative political and religious openness, regional political and religious movements had used Kuwait to establish media outlets over the past decade. I had seen some of these channels on screens in Bahrain and Saudi Arabia, and it was interesting that while some air Shia religious slogans others promote *salafi* religious messages.[14] But it was considered taboo in Kuwaiti media to discuss the protests and condemn the crackdown in Bahrain and particularly in Qatif. Both protest movements received only very limited attention on Gulf-owned channels such as Al-Jazeera and Al-Arabiya, and if they were reported, these channels usually focused on alleged Iranian meddling.[15] Hence, Gulf Shia would watch the Iranian-sponsored Arabic-language al-Alam channel, Lebanese Hizbullah's al-Manar, the Iraqi Ahlulbait television, pro-Assad Syrian channels or some of the Kuwaiti Shia channels. The new cold war in the Middle East turned into a full-fledged media war, in which media outlets were either with the protests in Bahrain and Qatif and for Assad's regime, or with the protests in Syria and against those in Bahrain and Qatif.

At the *diwaniyya* I also met Abd al-Hussayn al-Sultan, the editor-in-chief of the Kuwaiti newspaper *al-Dar* and a *shirazi* activist.

The newspaper *al-Dar* and the TV channel al-'Adala were new media outlets that catered to the Shia community. They were founded by Shia businessmen, who had expanded their business and media empires under Prime Minister Nasser al-Muhammad al-Sabah.[16] As al-Sultan told me, *al-Dar* had been temporarily suspended for reporting about the protests in Bahrain and Qatif in Spring 2012, and would be closed down for good by the end of 2012. In a similar vein, a Kuwaiti Shia was even sentenced to ten years in prison for his tweets critical of the ruling families of Bahrain and Saudi Arabia, as well as for allegedly insulting the prophet Muhammad and Aisha, one of the prophet's wives.[17]

This polarization of Middle Eastern media hardened people's perceptions of a sectarian divide. Most Kuwaiti Shia I met adopted the narrative portrayed in Shia- or Iranian-funded media that the Syrian uprising is just a Western plot funded by the Gulf states. They largely supported the regime of Bashar al-Assad, and nurtured deep suspicions toward the intentions and makeup of the Syrian opposition, while Sunnis would often say the exact opposite. Sectarianism also became a campaign tool for prospective *salafi* and Shia MPs. One man, who had just been elected an MP in the February 2012 elections, seemed to personify the new sectarian Gulf and all its contradictions: Abd al-Hamid Dashti.[18] Dashti is a prime example of a Shia identity entrepreneur, who tries to profit from a strengthened Shia identity in the region and has written a short history of the Shia in the Gulf.[19] But he has become such a controversial figure mainly because he strongly supported the protests in Bahrain and headed a Bahrain solidarity group in Kuwait. He was in touch with all sectors of the Bahraini opposition and during February and March 2011 tried to mediate an agreement between the opposition and the regime there. At the same time, however, he kept business ties with people close to the Syrian regime and even organized an event at which money for Bashar al-Assad's regime was collected in Kuwait, an act that was seen as hostile by the Syrian opposition and many Sunnis in Kuwait.[20]

But Sunni-Shia relations in Kuwait had not historically been as problematic as in most neighboring states. In fact, the al-Sabah ruling family has had a traditional alliance with the Shia merchant families, several of whom have created huge business conglomerates and amassed large amounts of wealth, and the al-Sabah have repeatedly used the Shia merchants as a counterweight to the Arab nationalist-leaning Sunni merchant elite.[21]

Nothing better displays the relationship between the old Sunni and Shia families in Kuwait than a drive through Kuwait City, through the neighborhoods of Bneid el-Gar and Sharq. Old buildings are slowly but steadily being replaced by skyscrapers, but right next to the old palace of the ruling family stand the houses of wealthy Shia merchant families, some of whom hailed from Iran and who contributed to Kuwait's cosmopolitan society. If one drives out into these neighborhoods immediately adjacent to downtown, large Shia mourning houses are built alongside *Diwans* from wealthy Shia and Sunni families. Some of these are large buildings that tower over major traffic intersections.

Unlike the Shia in Bahrain and the Eastern Province, who all claim to be the original inhabitants of their areas, Kuwaitis of all persuasions hail from somewhere else and mainly settled in the region over the past two centuries, chiefly for economic and political reasons. Hence, Kuwait could be called an immigrant society, in which the different groups retained features of their previous identities while also coming together as part of something new.[22]

But a country that is, as one Kuwaiti described it to me, "sandwiched" in between Iran, Iraq, and Saudi Arabia cannot escape the political developments in these countries. The Iranian Revolution and Iran's attempt to export the revolution, and a bombing campaign carried out by Shia activists based in Kuwait in the 1980s, all fueled sectarian animosities in the country.[23] Likewise, parts of the Sunni communities in Kuwait became radicalized, and anti-Shia rhetoric started to become more widespread. The Saudi-Iranian rivalry and the rise of Iraqi Shia after the Iraq War all left their mark, as did the rise of both Sunni and Shia Islamists in Kuwait, for whom doctrinal differences were important.[24] As regional tensions increased, sectarianism became more openly displayed in Kuwaiti politics, and it started to be used by sectarian identity entrepreneurs and political groupings to further their interests.

A key factor in the rise of sectarianism in Kuwait was the "Mughniya issue." After the military commander of Lebanese Hizbullah Imad Mughniya was assassinated in Damascus on February 12, 2008, two Kuwaiti Shia MPs from the Kuwaiti branch of the transnational Hizbullah networks and some other prominent Shia decided to mourn his death in public.[25] Mughniya is a persona non grata amongst most Sunni Kuwaitis, who accuse him of having hijacked a Kuwait Airways airliner in 1988 to secure the release of Shia prisoners in Kuwait.[26] After the funeral the two MPs were expelled from a cross-sectarian opposition alliance, the Popular Action Bloc.[27] They henceforth allied themselves with Prime Minister Nasser al-Muhammad al-Sabah, who was being challenged by the opposition in parliament and had long had strong ties with Kuwaiti Shia merchant families.[28]

This alliance ensured that when the youth movement against the prime minister started in earnest in 2009, and was given new impetus by the Arab Spring, the Shia political elite stood firmly with the prime minister and the al-Sabah ruling family. The ruling family increasingly labeled the protest movement as a tribal uprising against the sedentary people of Kuwait. While a majority of those opposing the ruling family are Islamists and belong to tribes, it would be too simplistic to view the opposition just through this lens. The struggle in Kuwait is mainly between a population that wants more political say and economic justice, and a ruling family and an oligarchy bent on trying to prevent just that. And the youth movement that has emerged as a strong force in Kuwaiti politics over the past few years has accelerated that struggle, seeking to speed up political change to a full constitutional monarchy, in which the ruling family would give up many of its political powers. While the Arab Spring has given new impetus to the youth movement, the Kuwaiti youth activists argue that their movement predated the Arab Spring, that it started in 2006. In 2005 and 2006, a so-called Orange Movement, named after the orange flags and T-shirts worn by protesters, fought for the right of women to vote and the reduction of the number of electoral constituencies from twenty-five to five, in an effort to curb alleged election rigging that benefited pro-ruling family candidates in the smaller constituencies. The protest movement, led in part by some of the same youth activists as today, succeeded, and the government had to concede these demands.[29] In reminiscence of this earlier mobilization, Orange flags again became the key marker of the Kuwaiti protests in 2011 and 2012.

Thereafter, the youth movement decided to focus on another main goal from October 2009 forward: the removal of the unelected prime minister Nasser al-Muhammad al-Sabah. The slogan *Irhal*, "get lost," became a rallying cry, and Kuwaiti activists claim that they had coined this term before it became a key slogan in the Tunisian and Egyptian revolutions in 2011.[30]

In early 2011, a new informal youth group was formed, calling itself *al-Sur al-Khamis*, the Fifth Wall, in a reference to the four walls that had protected the old city of Kuwait from attacks. It sought to intensify the campaign against the prime minister and for political reforms. This group was formed after some opposition MPs were beaten during an attack by security forces on a gathering at the *diwaniyya* of former Muslim Brotherhood MP Jama'an al-Hirbish. Many Kuwaiti activists have told me that this was a wake-up call for them, as it showed that the regime was willing to use limited violence to undermine its opponents. As Kuwaiti youth activists and former opposition MPs proudly relate, the attack on December 8, 2010, predated the self-immolation of Muhammad Bouazizi that set off the Tunisian Revolution by nine days. By making that analogy, they emphasize the importance of domestic factors for the mass mobilization Kuwait has since seen.[31]

Protest on Irada Square in front of the National Assembly, the Kuwaiti parliament, Kuwait City, on November 21, 2011. Photo by a local photographer who wishes to remain anonymous.

So over the past few years youths have become a powerful force in Kuwaiti politics that has undermined some established political groupings while making alliances with others. Key activists, for example, stem from the youth branch of the Muslim Brotherhood, while many are members of some powerful tribes.[32] In early 2011, a number of youth activists established a political group for youths, the Civil Democratic Movement, which calls for a constitutional monarchy.[33]

Protests gained pace throughout 2011, and things came to a head in November 2011 when youth activists stormed the Kuwaiti parliament in a protest against the government. This led a few days later to the resignation of the Kuwaiti prime minister Nasser al-Muhammad al-Sabah. The context for the storming of the assembly had been allegations of wide-scale corruption and vote buying by the prime minister, and in the months that followed more details about large payments from the prime minister to a range of MPs surfaced in the Kuwaiti press.[34] After this success, the demands of the youth movement were taken on by the established opposition groups, particularly the Muslim Brotherhood and a number of independent politicians, who started calling for an elected prime minister, the legalization of political parties, and a full constitutional monarchy.[35]

Jabir al-Mubarak al-Sabah, a former minister of defense and first deputy prime minister, was appointed as the new prime minister. The aforementioned newly elected February 2012 parliament moved ahead on the corruption investigations, but according to one member of the "majority bloc," a "nasty plot" led to the dissolution of the parliament. In June, after just 120 days, the constitutional court declared the elections invalid, thereby dissolving the opposition-dominated parliament.[36] In response, tens of thousands participated in a rally that was held at Irada Square (the Square of "Popular" Will) in front of the National Assembly, the Kuwaiti parliament. Irada Square had become a symbol of the protest movement, not unlike Tahrir Square in Cairo or the Pearl

Roundabout in Manama, with a speaker's corner, tents, and large carpets to sit on, and at times daily gatherings.[37]

Kuwait's parliament—the most powerful in the Arab Gulf countries—and its relatively free media and tradition of political debate, above all in the *diwaniyyas*, distinguishes it from the other members of the GCC. Following a bargain between the wealthy merchant families and the al-Sabah ruling family, the amir granted Kuwait a parliament and a constitution in 1962, a year after the State of Kuwait was established and the British Protectorate over Kuwait ended. The amir, however, retains the right to dissolve parliament and has suspended it twice in 1976 and 1986.[38] Only the invasion of Kuwait by Saddam Hussein in 1990 proved to be a game changer. After the country was liberated from Iraqi occupation in the First Gulf War, the exiled Kuwaiti ruling family reached a deal with the opposition that turned Kuwait into a liberalized autocracy and the most progressive political system in the GCC. The Kuwaiti parliament and the constitution were reinstated. Parliamentary elections throughout the 1990s and the 2000s were genuine political contestations with sophisticated campaigning and large voter turnout.[39] But many Kuwaitis feel it is time to also demand an elected government and an elected prime minister.

As the year progressed, sectarian tensions increased and the long-standing political crisis climaxed. After dissolving the February 2012 parliament, the constitutional court reinstated the previous parliament that had existed before the February 2012 elections, but it never convened. In October the amir dissolved that parliament and called for new elections on December 1, 2012.[40] Outraged, several Kuwaiti opposition groups called for popular protests. A first large protest on October 15 at Irada Square was broken up by the security forces. Musallam al-Barrak, an opposition figure who had gained the most votes for a single candidate in the February 2012 elections, gave a fiery speech that publicly challenged the political authority of the amir. The amir then confronted the protesters directly on October 19, 2012. He described the protests as "chaotic sedition that could jeopardize our country (and) undermine our national unity" and decreed changes to the electoral law, limiting voters to being able to choose just one candidate instead of four as had previously been the case.[41] The opposition said this would give more chances to less popular candidates and would allow for more government interference. A coalition of opposition groups announced a boycott of the upcoming December 1 parliamentary elections. Two days later, on October 21, a massive protest first flocked toward Irada Square and was then redirected via the Dignity of a Nation Twitter account to various other areas of the capital, including to the Kuwait Towers, with numbers estimated between 50,000 and 150,000. This protest was the biggest in Kuwait's history, and protesters were attacked with rubber bullets and tear gas by security forces, leading to injuries and many arrests, including of some opposition figures and several members of the ruling family.[42] The following weeks were characterized by a deep polarization of Kuwaiti society over the future of the political system and more mass protests.[43] People went out into the streets again after al-Barrak was arrested on October 29 and charged with insulting the amir for the speech he had given on October 15. Subsequent protests led to his release.[44]

Bowing to popular pressure, the government allowed another huge demonstration with tens of thousands of participants on November 30, 2012, which called for the boycott of the parliamentary elections the following day.[45] In the elections, mainly Sunni Islamists, tribal leaders, and the nationalist opposition urged their supporters to abstain from voting. Due to the participation of the Shia, many of the *hadar* merchant families, and a number of smaller tribes loyal to the ruling family, participation in the parliamentary elections was almost 40 percent.[46] Shia parliamentarians clearly profited from the boycott of the Sunni Islamists, and took seventeen out of fifty seats. While this is roughly proportionate to their share of the population, this was more political representation than they ever had before.[47] While this affirmed their loyalty

Security forces shoot water cannons at stateless (*Bidun*) protesters demanding citizenship rights in "Freedom Square" in Timaa, Jahra, outside of Kuwait City, on December 19, 2011. Photo by a local photographer who wishes to remain anonymous.

to the ruling family, it played into the hands of Sunni hardliners, who denounced the Shia participation in the elections.[48]

The ruling family and the new parliament quickly resumed business as usual. In fact, many supporters of the new parliament argued that for the first time in many years, the appointed government could actually implement significant infrastructure projects, based on a national development plan, which hitherto had been delayed by a critical parliament.[49]

The opposition, on the other hand, boycotted and will remain outside the political process until new elections are called. It can make its voice heard only through street protests, through discussions in *diwaniyyas*, and on social media. In the aftermath of the elections, more protests were organized through the Dignity of a Nation Twitter account, including a large rally on December 8, 2012.[50] The youth movement organized a sleep-in at Irada square on December 15 to protest against the opening of the first session of the new parliament, but a heavy security presence forced the protesters to move to the banking quarter. The account has called for several rallies since, and vowed to continue as long as the parliament is in office. At the fifth Dignity of a Nation rally on January 6, the security forces quickly dispersed demonstrators. The sixth rally on January 13, 2013, was called in the Sabah Naser suburb, a stronghold of the oppositional tribes. The security forces did not intervene, and several thousand participated in the rally.[51] From December onward, some youth activists also started to move away from places such as Irada Square to hold nightly protests in residential areas, but security forces often moved in quickly to disperse the protesters. A number of youth activists have also been arrested and put on trial. So while repression has increased, the youth movement and the group of former MPs that made up the majority bloc in the February 2012 parliament continue to try to bring down the current parliament and government. While protests have become less frequent and smaller in Spring 2013, an alliance of youth groups and former MPs established a common opposition front in March 2013, the Popular Action Movement, with clear goals such as an elected government, a return to the old voting system, and the legalization of political parties.[52] The sentencing on April 15, 2013, of Musallam al-Barrak, one of the leaders of the new opposition front, to five years in jail for his November 2012 "We will not allow you" speech again brought thousands into the streets. These protests were broken up violently by the security forces.[53]

While these mass protests rocked Kuwait, and a stand-off over the December 2012 parliamentary elections polarized Kuwaiti society, large protests erupted in other parts of Kuwait. They happened in the shantytowns located just a fifteen-minute drive from Kuwait City, where the unpaved roads and crammed, tiny houses stand in starkest contrast to the skyscrapers of downtown Kuwait. These are some of the poorest areas in the Gulf, areas many Kuwaitis have never been to. They are the *Bidun*, the more than hundred thousand stateless people of Kuwait.[54] Most *Bidun* are former nomads who missed out on registering for Kuwaiti citizenship when Kuwait gained independence from Britain in 1961 and introduced Kuwaiti passports. The *Bidun*, who do not have passports and are banned from voting, from higher education and from many jobs and social services, want greater regulation of their situation and the benefits of Kuwaiti citizenship.[55] But their problem touches upon some of the key issues of Kuwaiti politics: political economy, the demonization of tribes in the media, and sectarianism. A former Sunni MP argued that around 45 percent of the *Bidun* are Shia.[56] *Bidun* rights activists, however, claim that there are more *Bidun*, and that the number of Shia amongst them might be as high as 60 percent, with many from Shia tribes originally from Iraq.[57] Even though the Shia are now allied with the ruling family, they are still often viewed with suspicion. A naturalization of the *Bidun* would therefore change the sectarian balance in Kuwait in favor of the Shia.

While the *Bidun* have long complained about their grievances and have held protests for years, the Arab Spring has given them new hope, and they have held regular large protests since 2011, particularly in their neighborhoods. The right to protest technically is enshrined in the Kuwaiti constitution, but it only applies to Kuwaiti citizens, and since the *Bidun* do not have citizenship they face potentially harsh sentences for participating in protests with Kuwaiti citizens. This kept the *Bidun* largely away from the Dignity of a Nation protests, although some *Bidun* activists participated. The *Bidun* protests at the periphery are also illegal and get cracked down on quickly, but protests are more difficult to repress and protesters can escape more easily from the security forces.[58] The *Bidun* activists trust neither the government nor the opposition and are becoming increasingly radicalized and frustrated by their situation.[59]

So the Kuwaiti situation differs from the regime-led sectarianism seen in Bahrain and Saudi Arabia, indicating the potential limits of sectarian rhetoric by the Gulf regimes. But the Kuwaiti ruling family and its supporters have come up with a similarly xenophobic narrative, albeit one that points the finger at the Muslim Brotherhood, the tribes, and to a certain extent also the *Bidun*. Kuwait has for decades been a testing ground for regional political reforms. Opponents of democratic change in other Gulf states often use the conflicts surrounding Kuwait's parliament to argue that democracy does not work in the Gulf. Advocates of democratization in the Gulf likewise look to Kuwait to make the opposite case, arguing that the political machinations of the ruling family undermine the functioning of the parliament.[60] The Kuwaiti opposition and the youth activists are well aware that they are fighting a larger struggle with ramifications across the Gulf. If Kuwait were to move in the direction of a real constitutional monarchy, this would set a precedent. They know, therefore, that they have to overcome opposition not only by the Kuwaiti ruling family but also by the other Gulf ruling families. The standoff between advocates of a constitutional monarchy and the ruling family and its allies will therefore intensify and is shaped by the realities of the sectarian Gulf that allow for the manipulation of sectarian and tribal identities.

7 ARAB SPRINGS, ARAB FALLS

"From Oman to Bahrain, one people, not two."

—Protest chant in front of Bahraini embassy
in Muscat, Oman, March 19, 2011[1]

"Where is Democracy?"
"No to Corruption!"

—Protesters' slogans, Muscat, Oman, February 18, 2011[2]

"Knowing that those that satisfy themselves and upset their people tomorrow will have someone else sitting in their seat, for those that think the country is in your and your kids' names, the country is for the people, and its glories are theirs. Repeat with one voice, for one faith: We are all Tunisia in the face of repressive elites. . . . The Arab governments and who rules them are, without exception, thieves."

—Muhammad ibn al-Dhib al-Ajami, Qatari poet, 2011[3]

Across the Gulf, regimes suppressed calls for democracy, freedom, and dignity with a sectarian rhetoric and by accusing protesters of having a foreign agenda to delegitimize protest movements. And this has had repercussions beyond Bahrain, Saudi Arabia, and

Kuwait—in the UAE, Qatar, and Oman as well as in Syria, Iraq, Lebanon, and Iran. A sectarian Gulf worked both internally and externally as a divisive force and as a legitimizing tool for the GCC monarchies. Saudi Arabia and the UAE sent the biggest contingents to Bahrain as part of the Peninsula Shield Force in mid-March 2011. Even though other Gulf countries, particularly Oman and Kuwait, were hesitant, the move eventually was backed by all GCC member states due to Saudi pressure.[4] Driven by the sectarian logic and the ultimate goal of regime survival, the Gulf states shaped the Arab Fall and became key in the counter-revolution across the region. Internally, sectarianism has divided protest movements. Externally, it has served to isolate Iran and mobilize the Sunnis across the region against Iran and the Assad regime in Syria.

But in all Arab societies public criticism of rulers has become much more widespread. While this criticism varies from country to country, the language is transnational and is transmitted throughout the Arab world by satellite television, newspapers, and social media. A peculiarity of the Gulf is that social media were used by protesters as well as by regimes, arguably even more so than in Egypt, Tunisia, or Syria. Given the wealth and high standard of living across the region, almost every *Khaliji* has a smartphone and access to social media to spread news, debates, and protest announcements. In online discussions and in the streets, the ruling families of the region have become vulnerable to public criticism. But Gulf regimes are increasingly clamping down on online discussions, and most GCC states have since 2011 handed down year-long jail sentences for statements posted on social media or other websites that were deemed either insulting to the rulers or blasphemous.[5] While as of 2013 the Gulf regimes are still in power, this criticism has become widespread and many citizens have started to call for the establishment of a constitutional monarchy or the removal of the Gulf ruling families.

In Bahrain and in many areas of the Saudi Eastern Province, slogans and graffiti calling for the downfall or even death of the

Al Khalifa and Al Saud ruling families are common. In Kuwait, a broad alliance of youth activists, Sunni tribal politicians, *salafis*, and Muslim Brothers has become ever more critical of the ruling al-Sabah family, going so far as to attack the amir himself.

Even in Oman, which arguably has been ruled in the most absolutist fashion of all the Gulf states, the taboo of criticizing the sultan has been broken. Oman was the first Gulf country to experience popular protests in January 2011. From January until April 2011 protests quickly spread across the country. There were demonstrations and strikes in most Omani urban centers, starting in the northern industrial town of Sohar and then quickly spreading to Muscat, as well as Sur and the southern province of Dhufar, which had seen a rebellion in the 1960s and 1970s.[6] Protests were particularly intense in Sohar, where huge development projects centered around a new industrial port had taken place in recent years. Soharis complained that these industries provided few jobs while polluting the town and leading to a fall in groundwater levels. Protests in Sohar sparked off after young unemployed people were told that there would be no job opportunities for them in the local branch of the Ministry of Manpower.[7]

The iconic Globe Roundabout in Sohar on the main Muscat-Dubai highway became the venue of protests, and was dubbed "Reform Square." Protesters in Sohar attacked the local governor's office, a police station, and a large supermarket that were all adjacent to the square.[8] After two protesters were killed, the sultan apparently gave orders that protesters should be allowed to gather without being attacked. Contrary to demands in other Arab Spring protests, protesters had a largely reform-oriented agenda, demanding greater economic justice, improved living standards, an end to corruption, and the firing of several ministers, as well as political and constitutional reforms.[9] Unlike his Bahraini and Saudi counterparts, the sultan of Oman reacted to some of these demands early on, particularly to those that would not fundamentally alter the political system. He dismissed large parts of the cabinet, announced the creation of fifty thousand new public sector jobs, and raised the minimum salary. He also extended the powers of the advisory council, the Majlis al-Shura, and in new elections held in October 2011 several protest leaders were elected and the council did take up some of the protesters' demands.[10] He thereby temporarily satisfied the workers and the unemployed, who had been key constituents of the protests. As they increasingly stayed home, and mainly the urban intellectuals returned to the protest venues in Sohar, Muscat, and Dhofar, the security forces cracked down and arrested those calling for significant political reforms.[11] The actions of the government therefore undermined an alliance of workers and intellectuals who had been driving the protests. While the protests failed to develop into a sustained uprising, the profound challenge to the political system and the precedent of street politics and popular demands have undermined the authority and legitimacy of the political system, and thereby also of the sultan.[12]

But the Omani government did not use the kind of sectarian rhetoric endorsed in Bahrain and Saudi Arabia to divide protesters. Indeed, it seems to be in the government's interest to keep discussions of sectarian and ethnic divisions to a minimum, so as not to upset the delicate communal balance in the country. Sultan Qaboos is an *Ibadi* and not a Sunni Muslim. The *Ibadiyya* is a distinct sect that is separate from the Sunni and Shia schools of Islamic jurisprudence, and *Ibadis* constitute at least half the population of Oman. The rest mostly are Sunnis while a small percentage are Shia.[13] Apart from the role of the *Ibadiyya* in Oman, Shia and Hindu businessmen are very prominent in Omani politics and the economy. These include the Shia of Indian origin, the *Lawatiyya*,[14] who once held several key ministries, the most prominent example of whom was long-time minister of trade and industry Maqbool bin Ali bin Sultan. The 2011 protests were largely directed against an oligarchy perceived as corrupt and misleading the country, and some of the protest slogans had sectarian overtones, arguing that minorities, in other words, the Shia, were controlling the state and the economy.[15] But the sectarian fallout from the Bahrain uprising had repercussions in Oman. The two main Twelver Shia minorities in Oman, the *Lawatiyya* and particularly the *Baharna*, Shia of Bahraini origin, were initially sympathetic to the Bahrain uprising. They held small demonstrations in front of the Bahraini embassy in Muscat, particularly after the crackdown started in Bahrain in mid-March 2011.[16] In response to the protests calling for reform in Oman, the Shia notables got both communities to show solidarity and hold rallies in support of the sultan.[17] Protests erupted mainly in areas with Sunni inhabitants, as well as in the capital, while they were absent in the *Ibadi* heartland around Nizwa in the interior of Oman. But many *Ibadis* protested in Muscat, and the lack of protests in the interior is also a result of the historical trauma of the 1950s war that destroyed the independent imamate there, the *Ibadi* state, and serves as a reminder that the sultans of Muscat can use violence if they are challenged.[18]

So while the protest movement largely lost its appeal by mid-2011, discontent did not subside in Oman, and many of the economic measures taken by the government seem intended to appease the population in the short term rather than to solve the underlying economic and political problems that led to the protests. This was evident in a strike by oil workers in May and June 2012. Three bloggers who traveled to the oilfields and were covering the strike were arrested. To protest their detention, several dozen protested in Muscat, and they also were arrested and put on trial, and eventually given mostly one-year sentences. Those arrested included key figures who had been driving the protest movement in 2011, including Said Sultan al-Hashimi.[19] He had just finished editing a book with contributions by major Omani writers, academics, and activists on the "Omani Spring."[20]

While these activists were pardoned in March 2013 after going on a hunger strike to protest the procedures of their trial, their imprisonment did have the desired effect of reinstating a climate of fear in Oman, where everyone who criticized the government and particularly the Sultan could face serious consequences.[21] And the Omani government took inspiration from the destruction of the Pearl Monument in Bahrain and bulldozed the Globe Roundabout, the venue of protests in Sohar, to the ground. To erase the memory of the protests there, a large flyover was built over the roundabout, while many adjacent buildings were transformed so as to completely reshape the geography of the place.[22]

While the UAE did not see street demonstrations, petitions for political reform circulated there in 2011, and the state reacted with a campaign of repression against political and human rights activists, as well as handouts of wealth and an increase in salaries to government employees.[23] A petition signed by 132 Emiratis was released on March 3, 2011, calling for a fully elected parliament and a move toward constitutional monarchy.[24] Five of the signatories, dubbed the UAE five, were subsequently imprisoned. Several of them had managed a popular Emirati online discussion forum that in 2009 and 2010 had served as a platform to circumvent the UAE's tight restrictions on the media and free speech, and where criticism of government policies and the ruling families were widespread.[25]

The UAE's crackdown also specifically targeted local sympathizers of the Muslim Brotherhood, in a sign that the UAE rulers were deeply concerned that the Gulf branches of the Muslim Brotherhood may be inspired by their Egyptian, Tunisian, and Syrian counterparts to demand more political powers. The crackdown particularly aimed at the Association for Reform and Social Guidance, an Islamic movement dating back to the 1970s. Some of its leaders were arrested, while others were stripped of their nationalities.[26] The total number of arrested reached ninety-four by April 2013 and included well-known human rights activists and academics. Observers were kept away from a trial against those charged with subversion at the behest of the Muslim Brotherhood.[27]

Many of the arrested political activists stem from the poorer northern emirates such as Ras al-Khaimah, Sharjah, Ajman, and

Umm al-Qaiwain, where residents complain of being neglected in public services and infrastructure vis-a-vis the two glitzy emirates of Dubai and Abu Dhabi.[28] With his outspoken views and statements, Dubai's police chief, Dahi Khalfan, has become the mouthpiece of the anti–Muslim Brotherhood campaign in the Gulf.[29] Muslim Brotherhood activists in the region allege that the UAE's anti–Muslim Brotherhood stance is also influenced by the close relationship of the UAE with key members from the regime of former Egyptian president Hosni Mubarak.[30] The most prominent example of this is former prime minister Ahmad Shafiq, who after losing the presidential elections in 2012 against Muhammad Mursi went to the UAE into exile to escape corruption charges in Egypt.[31]

Economically, the UAE and Qatar profited from an increase in mainly Saudi tourists, who avoided Bahrain, and by the influx of businesses that relocated some of their staff from Bahrain to Dubai, Abu Dhabi, and Doha.[32] Mohammed bin Rashid al-Maktoum, prime minister of the UAE and the ruler of Dubai, even put a figure on the funds that fled Arab countries that experienced uprisings to the UAE when he stated, "We received 30 billion dirhams from the Arab Spring . . . plus/minus."[33] Together with sky-high oil prices, this actually led to a new kind of economic boom in the UAE and Qatar, even though this was overshadowed by the global financial crisis.[34]

The main Al-Jazeera channel and two special Al-Jazeera channels that focused chiefly on the Arab Spring protests became key drivers of the protests, particularly of those that led to the fall of Mubarak in early 2011. This was at odds with the Saudi position and the coverage of the Saudi-owned Al-Arabiya channel. Qatar saw the Arab Spring as an opportunity to assert its leadership role in the Arab world.[35] In 2011, Qatar helped the Libyan rebels early on, both logistically and militarily, establishing Doha as a new major center of diplomacy. Through their fighter jets, Qatar and the UAE were the only two Arab countries officially involved in the NATO intervention in Libya. Qatar also sent special forces to fight alongside Libyan revolutionaries.[36]

Qatar supported all the Arab protest movements, except in the Gulf states, and sought to back Islamist movements with ties to the Muslim Brotherhood and at times also the *salafis*. Qatar has therefore become popular amongst Islamists in the region, while more secular forces question Qatar's motives.[37]

But the protests in Bahrain, and the prospect that the ruling family there might lose control and the Shia might have more political power, shocked the Qatari ruling family, and Qatar supported the GCC-led intervention in Bahrain and sent in a symbolic troop detachment.[38] Yusuf al-Qaradawi, an Egyptian scholar with roots in the Muslim Brotherhood, who resides in Qatar, has become probably the most famous Islamic scholar in the Arab world through his television show on Al-Jazeera. While he strongly supported all the Arab uprisings outside of the Gulf, he called the protests in the Gulf "sectarian."[39]

Yet, even Qatar faces social tensions and domestic calls for political reform.[40] A group of Qataris led by a long-standing former Baathist opposition activist, Ali al-Kuwari, has been holding monthly political meetings in Qatar since March 2011 and published a book titled *The People Want Reform in Qatar . . . Also*. In the book al-Kuwari and his group ask for fundamental political reforms in Qatar.[41] Mohamed Althani, a member of the Qatari ruling family and a former minister of economy and trade (2004–2006) published a book in which he called for gradual political reform in the Gulf initiated by enlightened elites in order to prevent Arab Spring–style protests forcing change upon the Gulf region.[42] Particularly in the smaller Gulf states such as Qatar and the UAE, citizens voiced dissatisfaction with the high percentage of expatriates, and with the Western style of life that dominates the cities.[43]

Qatar, too, has proven that it will repress domestic criticism. Muhammad ibn al-Dhib al-Ajami, a Qatari poet, was sentenced to life imprisonment in November 2012 for a poem lauding the ideals of the Arab Spring and implicitly criticizing the Gulf rulers, proclaiming, "We are all Tunisia in the face of repressive elites."[44]

The message to other Qataris was clear. Amidst these calls for political reform at home, Qatar announced partial elections for the Consultative Council, but it was not clear when elections would be held and whether the council would have legislative powers.[45]

With mass protests in Bahrain in spring 2011, and smaller protest movements in Saudi Arabia, Oman, and Kuwait, the GCC states decided on a cotmmon strategy toward the Arab Spring abroad and the protests at home: protests in other Arab states could be supported if this served geopolitical interests, but there was zero tolerance for protests or demands for reform at home, where security and stability remained priority number one. But beyond the general sense that no ruling family in the GCC should lose its power, there were differences over how this should be achieved.

While all the GCC states adopted the logic of the sectarian Gulf, not all these states necessarily want to confront Iran. In fact, there are severe disagreements over foreign policies toward Iran.[46] Oman, for example, shares the Strait of Hormuz with Iran. This is a major reason why its good relations with Iran have continued after the Iranian Revolution.[47] Qatar, too, has tried to maintain positive relations with Iran, largely because Iran and Qatar share the world's biggest gas field, called North Field in Qatar and South Pars in Iran. However, the belligerent Qatari stance on Syria has put this alliance at risk.[48] In addition, some emirates depend on trade with Iran and are therefore vulnerable to the sanctions against Iran that the United States has worked hard to implement over the past years.[49]

Nevertheless, regime responses across the Gulf looked much alike. At home, foreign agents were blamed for the protests, generally a reference to Iran or the Muslim Brotherhood. The accusation that protests were foreign-inspired was also used in Oman. There, however, foreign support often refers to alleged Emirati support, and the Omani authorities announced they had uncovered an Emirati spy ring that had penetrated Sultan Qaboos' inner circle in January 2011.[50]

The Gulf states then became key in how the Arab Spring developed, and took up opportunities that political turmoil in other Arab states offered them. Much like in the Arab cold war in the 1950s and 1960s between conservatives and revolutionary states, the post-2011 Middle East became an arena for "competitive meddling" by "would-be regional powers" trying to influence the Arab public sphere.[51]

In trying to navigate the Arab Spring abroad, several GCC states supported Sunni Islamists in Tunisia, Libya, Egypt, and Syria. This support mainly went to *salafi* groups, while Qatar mainly backed the Muslim Brotherhood. Saudi Arabia was especially worried that a Muslim Brotherhood–dominated state could become a rival model for a Sunni Islamic state, and so sought to back *salafi* groups that were closer to its *Wahhabi* ideology.[52] The election of the Muslim Brotherhood candidate Muhammad Mursi as president of Egypt was seen as problematic by some Gulf states because of their fear of Muslim Brotherhood branches in the Gulf.[53]

Mursi's first foreign trip as president brought him to Saudi Arabia to meet King Abdullah in July 2012.[54] Saudi Arabia thought it was better to engage him so as not to drive him closer to Iran or to the revolutionary youth, who see Saudi Arabia in a negative light. Indeed, throughout the revolutionary process in Egypt, there were repeated protests in front of the Saudi embassy against the Saudi regime and its support for the counter-revolutionary forces in the region.[55] This Gulf pressure ensured that the newly elected Egyptian president did not move too close to the Iranians. Mursi was the first Egyptian president to visit Iran since the Iranian Revolution—to attend a meeting of the Non-Aligned Movement. But when he gave a speech in Tehran on August 30, 2012, he fell out with the Iranians over the Syrian uprising because he described it as part of the Arab Spring protests. He thereby contradicted the official rhetoric of the Iranians, who backed protests in Bahrain but not in Syria, their ally. An Iranian television channel even replaced the word *Syria* with *Bahrain* in a Persian translation of Mursi's speech praising the struggle for justice of the "Syrian people," leading to an uproar in Arab media and a diplomatic complaint from Manama.[56]

After Bahrain in early 2011, the uprising in Syria had the strongest impact on sectarian relations in the Gulf and the wider Middle East. Indeed, Syria became the mirror image of the Bahrain uprising, where Sunnis from the Gulf found a way of endorsing a revolution abroad while refraining from calling for one at home. Of course, this was very much part of calculated strategies by Gulf regimes in response to the Arab Spring, but it took on a dynamic beyond sheer government manipulation, and became a way for young *Khalijis* and the *salafis* and Muslim Brotherhood in the Gulf to jump on the bandwagon of revolutionary discourse.

Even Salman al-Awda, a former leader of the *Sahwa*, the Saudi Islamist opposition movement that emerged after the 1990–91 Gulf War, and one of the foremost Sunni Islamist critics of the Saudi government, argued that the Saudi government used the Syrian issue to position itself as a champion of revolutionary forces and not just the main actor of the Arab counter-revolution, all the while pursuing its strategic interests in the region.[57]

The protests in Syria were initially non-violent, sought political reforms, and were not driven by sectarian rhetoric. But much like in the Gulf states, the Syrian regime used the specter of civil war to scare Syria's minorities and ensure their loyalty, and used extreme violence early on to divide the protestors along sectarian and ethnic lines.[58] The uprising in Syria has gone on so long and has become so violent that it has hardened sectarian divisions in the region. The support the Syrian opposition gained from the Gulf states had repercussions for local politics in the Gulf states, and the decision to support the rebels was informed by the realities of the sectarian Gulf.

While the Gulf states initially were hesitant, they gave diplomatic, financial, and increasingly military support from mid- to late 2011 forward to the rebels.[59] Their hope is that a Sunni Islamist regime in Syria will be more sympathetic to the Gulf states, and will break the link between Iran, Syria, Hizbullah, and Hamas, and would in turn severely weaken Iran.

Consistent with the discourse of the sectarian Gulf, Gulf Islamist groups and donors framed their support for the Syrian uprising in sectarian terms, as a *jihad* against an infidel and Shia regime, supported by Iran. At the same time, Syrian rebel groups became more sectarian in their rhetoric. The logic goes that using sectarianism abroad will ensure at least temporary allegiance of the Sunni population in Syria to Gulf rulers. At the same time, it is thought to keep the Sunni and Shia Gulf citizens from uniting in calls for political reform in the Gulf states.

Four Bahraini *salafi* MPs, for example, traveled to Syria in August 2012 to publicly meet with leaders of the Free Syrian Army in a show of support. One of them, Abd al-Halim Murad, argued on Twitter that his visit was in support of the revolutionaries in their fight against the "hated Safavids," a term referring to the Safavid Empire that ruled Iran and which is a derogatory description for the Shia.[60] Kuwaiti *jihadists* also entered Syria to fight with the rebels, as did groups of Saudis, Algerians, and Pakistanis.[61] Meanwhile, the ideological backing for the uprising in Syria has also partly been provided by the Gulf states, often with a sectarian overtone. Most prominent is Adnan al-Araur, a Syrian cleric, who fled to Saudi Arabia from his native city of Hama after an Islamist uprising there was brutally crushed in 1982. Through his appearances on al-Safa, a television channel based in Saudi Arabia, he has become something of a figurehead for the fighters inside Syria.[62] Even before the uprising, he had become prominent for his derogatory views about Shia Islam, and he continues to use sectarian language to garner support for the revolution in Syria. People like him are fueling sectarian tensions inside Syria and play into the hands of *salafi-jihadi* groups and al-Qaeda, as their rhetoric overlaps in many ways.[63]

In my conversations with Sunni *Khalijis*, the support for the Syrian uprising was genuinely felt and so important to them that one of the things they accused the Shia in their own countries of was not supporting the Syrian revolution. But Syria retains a special status for Gulf Shia because of Sayyida Zeinab, the suburb of Damascus that is home to a large shrine revered by Shia Muslims. Sayyida Zeinab was an important transnational Shia hub, a site for pilgrimage, political organization, publishing, and religious teaching, and also a place for the summer holidays. Since 2003, many Iraqi refugees have moved to Sayyida Zeinab, and the area had effectively become a Shia enclave, a place that many Damascenes or other Syrians did not visit and that the Syrian Islamist opposition would point to in order to prove their allegations that the regime of Bashar al-Assad was trying to convert the population to Shia Islam.[64] With the start of the uprising, and particularly since the rebels started fighting government troops in Damascus, many Shia residents fled, and repeatedly there were stories of Shia clerics and pilgrims, some allegedly Iranian agents, being kidnapped or killed.[65] Given the strategic location of the suburb in the battle for Damascus, and as a symbolic place for Shia muslims, Iraqi and Lebanese Shia militias have moved in to defend Sayyida Zeinab against the rebels.[66] The relatively few Twelver Shia in Syria then joined other minorities, such as the various Christian denominations, the Alawites, and the Kurds, that denounced the intentions of the Syrian rebels, particularly the Jabhat al-Nusra, and complained that they were using *jihadi* and Islamist rhetoric to legitimize their struggle against the "heretical" Assad regime.[67]

Hatred amongst opposition fighters against the Twelver Shia in Syria is even more pronounced than against the Alawites. This is partially to be explained by the sectarian rhetoric stoked up by preachers such as al-Araur, but also by the blind endorsement that Iran and Lebanese Hizbullah give to the Syrian regime, which enrages its opponents even further against Twelver Shia domestically.[68] The Shia in Sayyida Zeinab likewise saw themselves in a larger sectarian struggle engulfing the region, defending the suburb against the rebels, whom they called *Wahhabis*.[69] Indeed, the increased tension between national attachments and tribal, sectarian, and Islamist identities that cross national borders is one of the long-term consequences of the reactions of the Gulf states to the Arab Spring. Indeed, apart from religious links, tribal ties between Syrian tribes and distant relatives in the Gulf states are key for garnering support from Gulf governments and individuals there. In many cases, tribal ties also determine which group in Syria gets money.[70] The salience of these identities, and the fact that they have been variously used by governments in their response to the Arab Spring, threatens to tear apart the social fabric in the Gulf states and the wider Middle East, pitting neighbor against neighbor, dividing streets according to sect, ethnicity, or tribe, as had previously happened in Lebanon and Iraq.

In response to the support of the Gulf states for the opposition in Syria, the Syrian regime has tried to find ways of undermining the Gulf monarchies. It did so by covering the uprisings in Bahrain and the Eastern Province in pro-Assad media and through limited cyber-warfare, particularly directed against Gulf governments and activists and journalists based in the Gulf.[71]

As a state with a Shia majority and access to the Gulf, Iraq is now also firmly involved in the sectarian Gulf. The Bahrain crisis quickly became a tool in domestic Iraqi politics. Prime Minister Nuri al-Maliki and his al-Dawa party did little to help their co-religionists in Bahrain, and so other Iraqi Shia actors stepped in to fill the void and capitalize on the Bahraini and Eastern Province protests. Many of them are sectarian identity entrepreneurs themselves. Ahmad Chalabi, for example, suddenly spoke out in defense of Bahraini protesters.[72] The Sadr movement of Muqtada al-Sadr tried to mobilize in support of Bahrain.[73] Muhammad Taqi al-Mudarrisi, the spiritual leader of the *mudarrisiyya* who is based in the Iraqi Shia shrine city of Karbala, supported the Bahraini and Eastern Province protests together with his brother, Hadi al-Mudarrisi, as was discussed earlier in this book. Grand Ayatollah Ali al-Sistani, who rarely comments on foreign political issues and whom most Bahrainis follow as their *marji' al-taqlid*, condemned the crackdown on the Bahraini protesters in mid-March 2011, after Saudi troops had crossed the causeway.[74] All this further strained relations between the Gulf states and the Shia-dominated Iraqi government led by al-Maliki.[75]

Tensions between Sunnis and Shia in Iraq have risen since the start of the Arab Spring, and sectarian bombings and killings have again become more frequent. Iraqi Sunnis started to protest against al-Maliki's government, which had shown severe autocratic tendencies and was accused of corruption.[76] Qatar has supported Sunni actors in Iraq since before the start of the Arab Spring, and the Qatari prime minister accused the al-Maliki government of mistreating Iraq's Sunni minority. Al-Maliki's political arch-rival, Iraqi vice-president Tariq al-Hashimi, was given refuge in Qatar in 2012 after he was accused in December 2011 by the al-Maliki government of running death squads against the Iraqi Shia.[77]

Al-Maliki stood with the Assad regime in the Syrian uprising because of geopolitical considerations and fears that the uprising in Syria and the sectarian fallout in the Gulf could lead to a sectarian civil war across the region that would reignite the civil war in Iraq and undermine his government. At the same time, street protests against al-Maliki have intensified since December 2012, leading to mass protests and casualties amongst protesters in majority-Sunni provinces.[78] Dubbed the "Sunni spring" by some, these protests largely involved Sunnis protesting against the Shia-led government, even though some Shia groups such as the Sadr movement temporarily aligned themselves with the protesters.[79] As in Syria, Gulf media presented this as an uprising of the disenfranchised Sunnis against a dictatorial Shia government.

The Bahrain crisis also had an impact on the Gulf states' relations with Lebanon, where the Shia party Hizbullah dominated the government from January 2011 until March 2013. Several Gulf countries vowed to expel hundreds of Lebanese migrant workers accused of having links to Lebanese Hizbullah.[80] Bahrain took a lead in sending back several dozen Lebanese migrant workers shortly after the crackdown there in mid-March 2011. This neatly fit into the government narrative that the protests in Bahrain were merely a sectarian plot with foreign backing. The first Lebanese were expelled after Hasan Nasrallah, the general secretary of Lebanese Hizbullah, had backed the demands of the Bahraini opposition and condemned the GCC intervention in Bahrain.[81] When Michel Aoun, the Christian leader aligned with Hizbullah, denounced the lack of support from the international community for protesters in Bahrain, this led to a diplomatic crisis between the GCC and Lebanon.[82]

The temporary suspension after 2011 of flights from some Gulf countries such as Bahrain to countries with large Shia populations such as Iran, Iraq, and Lebanon symbolizes how physically unbridgeable the sectarian Gulf has become and how it has repercussions far beyond the Gulf states. The sectarian Gulf, then, shaped the Arab Fall.

CONCLUSION

The Arab Spring has led to the sectarian Gulf. Given the Gulf's strategic importance, and the vast oil wealth at the disposal of its rulers, Gulf politics will influence the future of the wider Middle East, and the relationships amongst Islamic sects across the world. Through their close alliance with the GCC states, the United States and EU member states have played a role in the creation of the sectarian Gulf. From the perspective of the United States, and by default also that of the Europeans, the main enemies in the contemporary Middle East are Iran and al-Qaeda. All policies are tailored around these two enemies, and the Gulf states, particularly Saudi Arabia, are given free rein in their internal affairs and their regional policies because they are in line with the United States on these two issues, and because of the steady supply of oil they provide. Therefore, the Gulf states are seen as key partners in containing the Arab Spring. Security concerns, the vested interests of Western security establishments, and business links with the GCC states, which became even more important since the start of the financial crisis in 2008, have made most Western leaders extremely risk averse in their policies toward the Arab Spring, and vulnerable to pressure by their allies in the Gulf.

Sectarianism therefore seems to be a short-term solution initiated by Gulf rulers and at least tacitly backed by the West to weather the storm of the Arab Spring and to further isolate Iran. While some such as the main Bahraini Shia political group al-Wifaq and the Bahraini crown prince, Salman bin Hamad Al Khalifa, in February and March 2011 tried to overcome the sectarian Gulf, sectarian identity entrepreneurs worked hard to strengthen sectarian boundaries. The rhetoric of the sectarian Gulf has given newfound powers and opportunities to these sectarian identity entrepreneurs, people whose political, social, and economic standing depends on the skillful manipulation of sectarian boundaries and who profit if these boundaries become the defining markers of a particular segment of society. The popularity of these sectarian identity entrepreneurs has skyrocketed, and they play a crucial role in exacerbating sectarian tensions. Once it is socially acceptable, sectarian discourse rapidly takes on a dynamic of its own and gets used by different actors for their own particular interests.

In an attempt to effectively institutionalize the sectarian Gulf, Saudi Arabia's King Abdullah in December 2011 proposed a closer Gulf Union. Saudi Arabia, Bahrain, and pro-Saudi branches of the other Gulf ruling families were enthusiastic about this. Supporters of the union in Bahrain hoped it would be announced soon. A Saudi-Bahrain merger, or a wider Gulf Union, seems to be a favorite solution for hardliners in the Saudi and Bahraini ruling families. It would ensure that there is no majority Shia state left in the GCC, as the new political entity's population would be counted as part of the Gulf Union. It would also ensure that none of the GCC states develops into a constitutional monarchy, so that there are no precedents of significant political reform in a GCC state.

Unsurprisingly, Bahraini Shia held massive rallies against the proposal and argued that it should be subject to a popular referendum.[1] Opposition from other GCC states, and particularly from Oman halted the project for the time being.[2] The UAE, Qatar, Oman, and Kuwait saw this as a Saudi-led effort at closer political and military cooperation, which would make Saudi Arabia even more dominant than it already is in the GCC, and many in these countries were afraid of a future under stronger Saudi domination.[3] Nevertheless, the GCC leaders signed a security agreement that is largely intended to stifle domestic dissent and allegedly includes a clause that allows one GCC state to take legal action against a citizen of another GCC state who has criticized the policies of the former.[4] The new security agreement was applied in the case of three Bahraini dissidents, who were extradited from Oman to Bahrain.[5]

The increasing repression and the stifling of free speech through draconian new laws is directed at the counter-example of political mobilization, one that is based on civil activism, democratic values, and the rule of law, a political culture that transcends ties of sect, ethnicity, or tribe that was embodied in the early phases of the protest movements in Tunisia, Egypt, Libya, Syria, Yemen, Bahrain, Kuwait, and Oman. As the processes of revolution and counter-revolution turned messy and bloody, and regimes fought back, this civic activism became sidelined in many instances, but it will not fade away for good. The processes set in motion by the Arab Spring then will be played out in the coming years.

One academic even argues that all the political and economic systems in the Gulf are unsustainable and will collapse soon.[6] The Arab Spring has shown how unpredictable political outcomes are, and the protests that occurred in the Gulf since early 2011 have been different from earlier popular mobilization and have been significantly more threatening to Gulf rulers. First of all, Gulf rulers have now been directly addressed and criticized in street protests, actions crossing a "red line" that had been largely observed before. In addition, established opposition movements that participated in the political process in Bahrain, Saudi Arabia, and Kuwait were challenged by a new wave of youth movements, whose demands and tactics were inspired by the Arab Spring. The emergence of these youth movements has changed the balance of power. Their demands were higher than those of the established opposition groups, and some of the latter were even decried by the youth groups as traitors for engaging with the regimes. This undermined the position of the main Shia party in Bahrain, al-Wifaq, the main Shia political network in Saudi Arabia, the *shirazis*, and some of the political groups and MPs in Kuwait. But the youth movements in Bahrain, Saudi Arabia, and Kuwait found allies in splinter groups of the main opposition groups and worked together with veteran opposition figures who embraced their high political demands. These became figureheads who were willing to cross red lines and pay the price of severe persecution to achieve political change.[7]

The Gulf monarchies have weathered the first storm of the Arab Spring through a mix of repression, handouts of wealth, and the creation of the sectarian Gulf. The handouts of wealth provided by the Gulf rulers at the beginning of the Arab Spring helped to keep the majority of citizens at home. But the theory of the rentier state, in which the state pays rents to its citizens while taxation is nonexistent and demands for democracy do not develop, has been refuted by the protests in the Gulf.[8] In addition, the ability by Gulf states to partially buy off opposition will in the coming decades be more limited than now. In many ways, the level of mobilization in Bahrain, where in the largest rallies up to a quarter of the citizen population was out in the street protesting against the government, is just a prelude to what might follow in the other GCC countries. The future of the Gulf will be inherently insecure, as most of the Gulf states have to manage the transition to a post-oil economy over the next decades.[9]

The problem is not just that in some states, such as Bahrain and Oman, the oil and gas reserves are declining rapidly.[10] In all the Gulf countries, domestic energy consumption has risen dramatically and the low prices ensure that energy is wasted on luxury. Saudi Arabia's domestic energy consumption, symbolized by Humvees, private planes, and cooled villas in the middle of the Arabian desert, is increasing steadily. In fact, if energy consumption continues to rise at current levels, Saudi Arabia may become a net importer of oil by 2030 because it needs so much of its oil to satisfy domestic energy demand.[11] But events since 2011 have also shown that the ways in which Gulf rulers have reacted to the Arab Spring have failed to satisfy the political demands of many Gulf citizens. The language of politics in the Gulf has changed profoundly. The Gulf ruling families try everything they can to block democratic transitions. But it remains to be seen whether they can carve out a solid position for themselves in the post–Arab Spring reality.

Sectarianism was a short-term "answer" to the Arab Spring in the Gulf. But the Gulf states will have to find new answers to the looming challenges of lack of economic diversification, increasing energy consumption, youth unemployment, and demands for political reform in an era and neighborhood in which autocratic regimes have lost the power to regulate what people say and demand in public. The youth activism, the mobilizing force of the Internet and smartphones, and the experience of the Arab Spring as the defining moment of a whole generation of young Arabs means that change has to come, be it through reform or, eventually, revolutionary outburst.

ACKNOWLEDGMENTS

Many people have contributed to this book, be it through participating in discussions, by helping me on fieldwork, by sharing contacts and sources, or by welcoming me in their countries. They are too numerous to all be mentioned, and the realities of the post–Arab Spring Middle East mean that many would like to stay anonymous so as not to face retribution. You know who you are, and it is to you that I dedicate this book.

I am extremely grateful to the following people for their help and for their comments on earlier versions of this manuscript:

Khaled Abdallah, Abdulnabi al-Akri, Louis Allday, Khadija von Zinnenburg Carroll, Chloe Nahum-Claudel, Kristin Smith Diwan, Joost Hiltermann, Claudia Honegger, Mansoor al-Jamri, Yusuf Khalfan, Laleh Khalili, David Kettler, Stéphane Lacroix, Laetitia Nanquette, Sajjad Rizvi, Adrian Ruprecht, Mahdi al-Salman, Tawfiq al-Sayf, Roger Tomkys, Kristian Coates Ulrichsen, Marc Valeri, Alice Wilson, and the two anonymous reviewers.

Kai Matthiesen has helped me at several stages, including with the visual aspects of the book. A special thank you goes to Mazen Mahdi from Bahrain, who has granted permission to use his pictures of the Bahrain uprising in the book, as well as to the anonymous photographers from Saudi Arabia and Kuwait who have kindly provided me with pictures.

It has been a great pleasure working with my editor, Kate Wahl, and her assistant, Frances Malcolm, at Stanford University Press. Kate has been everything one would hope for in an editor.

I would like to thank Pembroke College, University of Cambridge, for providing me with a working environment that enabled the writing of this book. Fieldwork for this book was funded by the British Institute for the Study of Iraq, the "Clerical Authority in Shi'ite Islam" project sponsored by the British Academy, and the London School of Economics and Political Science.

NOTES

All websites quoted in this book were last accessed on April 14, 2013, and updates for this book stopped in early April 2013.

PREFACE

1. Slavoj Žižek, *The Year of Dreaming Dangerously* (London: Verso, 2012).

2. David Graeber, *Inside Occupy* (Frankfurt a.M.: Campus Verlag, 2012), 11–15.

3. Sean L. Yom and F. Gregory Gause III, "Resilient Royals: How Arab Monarchies Hang On," *Journal of Democracy* 23, no. 4 (2012): 74–88.

4. The Gulf region is generally known as the *Persian Gulf.* Reflecting geopolitical tensions and ethnic divisions between the Arab Gulf states and Iran, however, the Gulf region is in the Arab world usually referred to as *Arabian Gulf.* It will be neutrally called *Gulf* in this book.

5. Saudi Arabia is the world's largest net exporter of oil, with an export of about eight million barrels a day in 2012, and holds a fifth of the world's proven oil reserves. U.S. Energy Information Administration (EIA), *Saudi Arabia Country Analysis Brief,* http://www.eia.gov/countries/country-data.cfm?fips=SA&trk=m.

6. "David Cameron on GP: 'Bahrain Is Not Syria'," BBC, April 20, 2012, http://www.bbc.co.uk/news/uk-17789082.

7. The notion of the entrepreneur who capitalizes on certain forms of identity formation is taken from the instrumentalist study of ethnicity, which argues that collective identities can be used as a political resource by competing interest groups. Paul R. Brass, *Ethnicity and Nationalism: Theory and Comparison* (London: Sage, 1991), 8. The concept has been termed "Shia ethnic entrepreneurs" in the case of Lebanese Shia. Roschanack Shaery-Eisenlohr, *Shi'ite Lebanon: Transnational Religion and the Making of National Identities* (New York: Columbia University Press, 2008), 6.

8. See, for example, Francis Fukuyama, *The End of History and the Last Man* (Harmondsworth: Penguin, 1993); Samuel P. Huntington, *The Clash of Civilizations and the Remaking of World Order* (New York: Simon & Schuster, 1997).

9. Vali Nasr, *The Shia Revival: How Conflicts Within Islam Will Shape the Future* (London: W.W. Norton, 2007).

10. Islamic history is, of course, more complex than that, and several Shia dynasties ruled different parts of the Islamic world at different times. See Ofra Bengio and Meir Litvak (eds.), *The Sunna and Shi'a in History: Division and Ecumenism in the Muslim Middle East* (New York: Palgrave Macmillan, 2011); Fuad I. Khuri, *Imams and Emirs: State, Religion and Sects in Islam* (London: Saqi, 1990).

11. See, among others, Juan Cole, *Sacred Space and Holy War: The Politics, Culture and History of Shi'ite Islam* (London: I.B. Tauris, 2002); and Rula Jurdi Abisaab, *Converting Persia: Religion and Power in the Safavid Empire* (London: I.B. Tauris, 2004).

12. Some see direct links between the Green Movement and the Arab Spring, and their mobilization strategies are remarkably similar. Hamid Dabashi, *The Arab Spring: The End of Postcolonialism* (London: Zed Books, 2012).

13. Out of a population of around eighty million, roughly 9 percent are Sunni and 2 percent are Arab. There are many Sunnis

amongst the Kurds, the Baluchs, the Turkomen, and the Arab minorities in Iran. The Iranian regime denies Sunnis some of their religious freedoms. "Sunni Muslims Banned from Holding Own Eid Prayers in Tehran," *The Guardian*, August 31, 2011, http://www.guardian.co.uk/world/2011/aug/31/iran-forbids-sunni-eid-prayers; Central Intelligence Agency, *The World Factbook: Iran*, September 12, 2012, https://www.cia.gov/library/publications/the-world-factbook/geos/ir.html; Rasmus Christian Elling, *Minorities in Iran: Nationalism and Ethnicity after Khomeini* (New York: Palgrave Macmillan, 2013). For online activism of Iranian Sunnis, see, for example, the Twitter account @Sunnis_Iran and http://en.sunnionline.us.

14. Human Rights Watch, *Iran: Halt Execution of Arab Activists: Five Men Sentenced to Death Following Closed Trials*, July 11, 2012, http://www.hrw.org/news/2012/07/11/iran-prevent-execution-arab-activists.

15. Author interviews with academics, politicians, and activists in Bahrain, Saudi Arabia, and Kuwait, 2011 and 2012.

16. "Iraqi Blast Damages Shia Shrine," BBC, February 22, 2006, http://news.bbc.co.uk/1/hi/world/middle_east/4738472.stm.

17. "The Bomb That Changed Iraq Forever," *The New York Times*, July 31, 2008, http://atwar.blogs.nytimes.com/2008/07/31/the-bomb-that-changed-iraq-forever; Fanar Haddad, *Sectarianism in Iraq: Antagonistic Visions of Unity* (London: Hurst & Company, 2011), 180f.

18. Qatar is the only member of the GCC that has openly backed Muslim Brotherhood branches across the region. This will be discussed later in the book.

19. See, for example, Ussama Samir Makdisi, *The Culture of Sectarianism: Community, History, and Violence in Nineteenth-Century Ottoman Lebanon* (Berkeley: University of California Press, 2000); Max Weiss, *In the Shadow of Sectarianism: Law, Shi'ism, and the Making of Modern Lebanon* (Cambridge, MA: Harvard University Press, 2010); Benjamin Thomas White, *The Emergence of Minorities*

in the Middle East: The Politics of Community in French Mandate Syria (Edinburgh: Edinburgh University Press, 2011).

20. Samir Khalaf, *Civil and Uncivil Violence in Lebanon: A History of the Internationalization of Communal Conflict* (New York: Columbia University Press, 2002).

21. Kuwait became independent in 1961. Gregory Gause III, *The International Relations of the Persian Gulf* (Cambridge: Cambridge University Press, 2010).

22. This is particularly strong amongst the Bahraini ruling family and partly stems from the fact that Iranian media such as the right-wing newspaper *Keyhan* occasionally refer to Bahrain as the fourteenth province of Iran. Bahrain has at different times in history been ruled from Iran, lastly under the Safavid Empire until the eighteenth century. Iran's historical claim over Iran was, however, given up by Shah Mohammed Reza Pahlavi in 1970, and a UN-administered opinion poll conducted the same year concluded that most Bahrainis, both Sunni and Shiite, wanted Bahrain to become an independent Arab state, rather than a province of Iran. International Crisis Group, *Popular Protests in North Africa and the Middle East (III): The Bahrain Revolt*, April 6, 2011, http:// www.crisisgroup.org/en/publication-type/media-releases/2011/ mena/the-bahrain-revolt.aspx, 11.

CHAPTER ONE

1. Population figures as of 2010. Pew Research Center, *The Future of the Global Muslim Population: Projections for 2010–2030*, January 2011, 14, 153f., http://www.pewforum.org/The-Future-of -the-Global-Muslim-Population.aspx.

2. See U.S. diplomatic cable released by Wikileaks: From Embassy Riyadh to Secretary of State, *Al-Hasa Shi'a Welcome U.S. Intervention in Iraq, Seek Improvements at Home,* January 3, 2006, 06RIYADH42, http://wikileaks.org/cable/2006/01/06RIYADH42.html.

3. For background on demographics and the political history of the Gulf Shia, see Graham E. Fuller and Rend Rahim Francke,

The Arab Shi'a: The Forgotten Muslims (New York: St. Martin's Press, 1999); Laurence Louër, *Transnational Shiite Politics: Religious and Political Networks in the Gulf* (New York: Columbia University Press, 2008); Yitzhak Nakash, *Reaching for Power: The Shi'a in the Modern Arab World* (Princeton, NJ: Princeton University Press, 2006); Michael Stephens, "Ashura in Qatar," *Open Democracy*, November 26, 2012, http://www.opendemocracy.net/michael-stephens/ashura-in-qatar.

4. Contemporary Saudi Arabia is also home to half a million Ismailis in Najran province bordering Yemen, as well as a hundred-thousand-strong indigenous Twelver Shia community in Medina, and hundreds of thousands of Shia living in the main urban centers of Riyadh and Jeddah due to internal migration.

5. Robert Vitalis, *America's Kingdom: Mythmaking on the Saudi Oil Frontier*, 2nd ed. (London: Verso, 2009).

6. These liberal enclaves draw the ire of the religious establishment. Ahmed Al Omran, "Party in the KSA," *Foreign Policy*, January 14, 2013, http://www.foreignpolicy.com/articles/2013/01/14/saudi_arabia_like_youve_never_seen_it_before.

7. For an account of the segregated realities experienced by Indian migrant workers in Bahrain, see Andrew M. Gardner, *City of Strangers: Gulf Migration and the Indian Community in Bahrain* (Ithaca, NY: Cornell University Press, 2010).

8. *The Independent* called the race "one of the most controversial in the history of the sport." "Rage Against the Formula One Machine," *The Independent*, Saturday, April 21, 2012, http://www.independent.co.uk/news/world/middle-east/rage-against-the-formula-one-machine-7665991.html. For the involvement of Gulf royals and investors with F1, see Christopher Davidson, *After the Sheikhs: The Coming Collapse of the Gulf Monarchies* (London: Hurst & Company, 2012), 92–93, 122, 206, 209.

9. See, for example, Stephen M. Walt, "Why the Tunisian Revolution Won't Spread," *Foreign Policy*, January 16, 2011, http://walt.foreignpolicy.com/posts/2011/01/15/why_the_tunisian_revolution_wont_spread.

10. International Crisis Group, *Popular Protests in North Africa and the Middle East (III): The Bahrain Revolt*, April 6, 2011, 3f., http://www.crisisgroup.org/en/publication-type/media-releases/2011/mena/the-bahrain-revolt.aspx; J. E. Peterson, "Bahrain: Reform, Promise and Reality," in *Political Liberalization in the Persian Gulf*, ed. Joshua Teitelbaum, 157–185 (New York: Columbia University Press, 2009).

11. Because the Salmaniya Medical Complex houses the main morgue in Bahrain, and dozens of people were killed and severely injured by the security forces in February and March 2011, protests and funeral processions regularly started at Salmaniya and there were protests outside the hospital. The regime later claimed that protesters had taken over the hospital and used it as a communications base for their planned "coup." The regime launched a massive media defamation campaign against medical personnel that treated wounded protesters at Salmaniya, and put several of them on trial. For a discussion of the events at Salmaniya, see Bahrain Independent Commission of Inquiry, *Report of the Bahrain Independent Commission of Inquiry*, November 23, 2011, 171–217, www.bici.org.bh. See also Doctors Without Borders, "Health Services Paralyzed: Bahrain's Military Crackdown on Patients," April 2011, http://www.doctorswithoutborders.org/publications/article.cfm?id=5171.

12. Nelida Fuccaro, *Histories of City and State in the Persian Gulf: Manama Since 1800* (Cambridge: Cambridge University Press, 2009); Fuad I. Khuri, *Tribe and State in Bahrain: The Transformation of Social and Political Authority in an Arab State* (Chicago: The University of Chicago Press, 1980); Emile A. Nakhleh, *Bahrain: Political Development in a Modernizing Society* (Lexington, MA: Lexington Books, 1976).

13. 'Abd al-Nabi al-'Akri, *al-tanzimat al-yasariyya fi al-jazira wa-l-khalij al-'arabi* (*The Leftist Organizations in the Peninsula and the Arabian Gulf*) (Beirut: Dar al-Kunuz al-Adabiyya, 2003).

14. National Democratic Action (*al-'amal al-watani al-dimuqrati*), known by its Arabic acronym Wa'ad (Promise).

15. The Islamic National Accord Association (*jama'iyyat al-wifaq al-watani al-islamiyya*), short al-Wifaq, was founded in 2001 as an umbrella group comprising three main Shia political and religious trends (al-Dawa Party, Hizbullah, and parts of the *shirazis*). These Shia groups will later be discussed in detail.

16. Marc Valeri, "Contentious Politics in Bahrain: Opposition Cooperation Between Regime Manipulation and Youth Radicalisation," in *The Dynamics of Opposition Cooperation in the Arab World: Contentious Politics in Times of Change*, ed. Hendrik Kraetzschmar, 129–149 (New York: Routledge, 2012).

17. Munira Fakhro, "The Uprising in Bahrain: An Assessment," in *The Persian Gulf at the Millennium: Essays in Politics, Economy, Security, and Religion*, ed. Gary Sick and Lawrence Potter, 167–188 (New York: St. Martin's Press, 1997); and Ute Meinel, *Die Intifada im Ölscheichtum Bahrain: Hintergründe des Aufbegehrens von 1994–1998* (Münster: Lit-Verlag, 2003).

18. Bahrain Independent Commission of Inquiry, *Report, 72f.*

19. Haqq Movement: Movement for Liberties and Democracy (*harakat haqq: harakat al-hurriyyat wa-l-dimuqratiyya*) and al-Wafa Islamic Trend (*tayyar al-wafa' al-islami*). By law Bahrain has no formal political parties, only political societies that effectively function as parties. These have to be registered with the government and can be dissolved. Haqq and al-Wafa refuse to be registered.

20. These were slogans using the term *vanguard*, as in vanguard youth (*shabab al-tali'a*), playing on the name of the old political movement of the *shirazis*, Movement of Vanguards' Missionaries (harakat al-risaliyyin al-tali'a). For background on the *shirazis*, particularly in Saudi Arabia, see Fouad Ibrahim, *The Shi'is of Saudi Arabia* (London: Saqi Books, 2006); Louër, *Transnational Shiite Politics*; Toby Matthiesen, *The Shia of Saudi Arabia: Identity Politics, Sectarianism and the Saudi State*, PhD dissertation, SOAS, 2011.

21. The *shirazis* in Bahrain are formally organized in the Islamic Action Society Amal (*jama'iyyat al-'amal al-islami*), which was banned in June 2012. For background on the different Shia political groups active in Bahrain and during the uprising, see International

Crisis Group, *Popular Protests in North Africa and the Middle East (III): The Bahrain Revolt*, April 6, 2011, http://www.crisisgroup.org/en/publication-type/media-releases/2011/mena/the-bahrain-revolt.aspx; ʿAbbas Mirza al-Mirshid and ʿAbd al-Hadi al-Khawaja, *al-tanzimat wa-l-jamaʿiyyat al-siyyasiyya fi al-Bahrayn* (*The Political Organizations and Groupings in Bahrain*) (Bahrain: Faradis lil-Nashr wa-l-Tawziʿ, 2008); Falah ʿAbdallah al-Mudayris, *al-harakat wa-l-jamaʿat al-siyyasiyya fi al-Bahrayn 1937–2002* (*The Political Movements and Groups in Bahrain 1937–2002*) (Beirut: Dar al-Kunuz al-Adabiyya, 2004); and Sajjad Rizvi, "Shiʿism in Bahrain: Marjaʾiyya and Politics," *Orient*, no. 4 (2009): 16–24.

22. Al-Jazeera English's coverage was better. *Shouting in the Dark*, a fifty-minute documentary about the uprising in Bahrain from the first days of the roundabout, was aired on August 4, 2011. It captures the spirit of the Pearl Roundabout exceptionally well, and also shows the brutal reality of the crackdown and explains the events at Salmaniya Medical Complex. While it caused a severe diplomatic crisis between Bahrain and Qatar, it was used by Al-Jazeera executives to claim that the network covered the Bahrain protests in a relatively objective manner. Contrary to Al-Jazeera Arabic, though, its English channel is much less influential and not directed at Arabs, and reporting on Bahrain on the English channel henceforth did not pose a similar threat. Interview with a senior Al-Jazeera executive, United Kingdom, November 2012. The documentary is available at http://www.aljazeera.com/programmes/2011/08/201184144547798162.html.

23. For a timeline of events during the February-March 2011 protests, see Bahrain Independent Commission of Inquiry, *Report, 65–169;* Cortni Kerr and Toby C. Jones, "Revolution Paused in Bahrain," *Middle East Report Online*, February 23, 2011, www.merip.org/mero/mero022311; Lin Noueihed and Alex Warren, *The Battle for the Arab Spring: Revolution, Counter-Revolution and the Making of a New Era* (New Haven, CT: Yale University Press, 2012), 135–163.

CHAPTER TWO

1. Quoted in "MOORE: Bahrain, a Vital U.S. Ally: Backing Protesters Would Betray a Friend and Harm American Security," *Washington Post*, November 30, 2011, http://www.washingtontimes.com/news/2011/nov/30/bahrain-a-vital-us-ally.

2. Madawi al-Rasheed, "Sectarianism as Counter-Revolution: Saudi Responses to the Arab Spring," *Studies in Ethnicity and Nationalism* 11, no. 3, (December 2011): 513–526.

3. Religious beliefs and practices, as well as places of worship, differ significantly between Twelver Shia and Alawites. While some Twelver Shia regard Alawites as heretics, others have accepted their beliefs as a valid form of Islam, and Alawites are in the media often presented as a Shia sect, since their teachings are closer to the mainstream Twelver Shia Islam than to Sunni Islam. Martin Kramer, "Syria's Alawis and Shi'ism," in *Shi'ism, Resistance, and Revolution*, ed. Martin Kramer, 237–254 (London: Westview, 1987).

4. "Shia-Fubiyya," *Al-Hayat*, August 31, 2012, http://alhayat.com/OpinionsDetails/430593.

5. See, for example, the statement by the Bahraini foreign minister in May 2012: "Bahrain Warns Iran Against Meddling in Its Affairs," Agence France-Presse, May 17, 2012, http://en-maktoob.news.yahoo.com/bahrain-warns-iran-against-meddling-affairs-141816264.html.

6. See Saeed M. Badeeb, *Saudi-Iranian Relations 1932–1982* (London: Saqi Books, 1993); Henner Fürtig, *Iran's Rivalry with Saudi Arabia Between the Gulf Wars* (Reading, UK: Ithaca Press, 2002); Christin Marschall, *Iran's Persian Gulf Policy: From Khomeini to Khatami* (London: Routledge, 2003); Frederic Wehrey, et al., *Saudi-Iranian Relations Since the Fall of Saddam: Rivalry, Cooperation, and Implications for U.S. Policy*, RAND National Security Research Division, 2009, http://www.rand.org/pubs/monographs/MG840.html.

7. For background, see Graham E. Fuller and Rend Rahim Francke, *The Arab Shi'a: The Forgotten Muslims* (New York: St. Martin's Press, 1999); Laurence Louër, *Transnational Shiite Politics: Religious*

and Political Networks in the Gulf (New York: Columbia University Press, 2008); Yitzhak Nakash, *Reaching for Power: The Shi'a in the Modern Arab World* (Princeton, NJ: Princeton University Press, 2006).

8. David Commins, *The Wahhabi Mission and Saudi Arabia* (London: I.B. Tauris, 2006); Natana J. DeLong-Bas, *Wahhabi Islam: From Revival and Reform to Global Jihad* (London: I.B. Tauris, 2007); Nabil Mouline, *Les clercs de l'Islam: autorité religieuse et pouvoir politique en Arabie Saoudite, XVIIIe–XXIe siècle* (Paris: Presses Universitaires de France, 2011).

9. Guido Steinberg, *Religion und Staat in Saudi-Arabien: Die wahhabitischen Gelehrten 1902–1953* (Würzburg: Ergon Verlag, 2002), 484–505.

10. See, for example, Guido Steinberg, "The Wahhabiyya and Shi'ism, from 1744/45 to 2008," in *The Sunna and Shi'a in History: Division and Ecumenism in the Muslim Middle East*, ed. Ofra Bengio and Meir Litvak, 163–182 (New York: Palgrave Macmillan, 2011); Guido Steinberg, "Jihadi-Salafism and the Shi'is: Remarks About the Intellectual Roots of Anti-Shi'ism," in *Global Salafism: Islam's New Religious Movement*, ed. Roel Meijer, 107–125 (London/New York: Hurst/Columbia University Press, 2009).

11. One of the most famous anti-Shia treatises from Saudi Arabia is Nasir ibn Sulayman al-'Umar, *waqi' al-rafida fi bilad al-tawhid* (The Situation of the Rejectionists in the Lands of Monotheism) (n.p.: n.d.), http://ar.islamway.net/book/3165. Written in 1993, it is a shallow analysis of the politics and religious rituals of the Shia inside Saudi Arabia, and brandishes them as infidels and a danger to the nation and the community of Muslim believers. See also Raihan Ismail, "The Saudi Ulema and the Shi'a of Saudi Arabia," *Journal of Shi'a Islamic Studies* 5, no. 4 (2012): 403–422.

12. This bargain was largely intact until 1979, when protests organized by the main Shia Islamist group in the region—the *shirazis*—revolted against the state's discrimination against the Shia as well as the complicity of their own elite in the state's policies.

For details on the 1913 agreement, see Hamza al-Hasan, *al-shiʻa fi al-mamlaka al-ʻarabiyya al-suʻudiyya* (The Shia in the Kingdom of Saudi Arabia), 2 vols., vol. 2 (Beirut: Muʼassasat al-Baqiʻ li-ʼIhiaʼ al-Turath, 1993), 12; Fouad Ibrahim, *The Shiʻis of Saudi Arabia*, (London: Saqi Books, 2006), 25; Toby Matthiesen, *The Shia of Saudi Arabia: Identity Politics, Sectarianism and the Saudi State*, PhD dissertation, SOAS, 2011, 127f.

13. Through labor migration to the Eastern Province, the Shia ceased to be a clear majority in the province, but continue to make up roughly half of the population there.

14. The attackers, led by Juhayman al-ʻUtaybi, held out in the Grand Mosque of Mecca for three weeks. Even though observers at the time thought differently, the al-ʻUtaybi group was unrelated to the Shia uprising and was made up of dissatisfied tribal elements and former National Guard officials. Thomas Hegghammer and Stéphane Lacroix, "Rejectionist Islamism in Saudi Arabia: The Story of Juhayman al-ʻUtaybi Revisited," *International Journal of Middle East Studies* 39, no. 1 (2007): 103–122; Yaroslav Trofimov, *The Siege of Mecca: The Forgotten Uprising* (London: Allen Lane, 2007).

15. Toby Craig Jones, *Desert Kingdom: How Oil and Water Forged Modern Saudi Arabia* (Cambridge, MA: Harvard University Press, 2010), 179–216.

16. Joseph Kostiner, "Shiʼi Unrest in the Gulf," in *Shiʼism, Resistance, and Revolution*, ed. Martin Kramer, 173–186 (Boulder, CO: Westview Press, 1987).

17. Mamoun Fandy, *Saudi Arabia and the Politics of Dissent* (Basingstoke: Palgrave, 1999); Stéphane Lacroix, *Awakening Islam: The Politics of Religious Dissent in Contemporary Saudi Arabia* (Cambridge, MA: Harvard University Press, 2011); Madawi al-Rasheed, *Contesting the Saudi State: Islamic Voices from a New Generation* (Cambridge: Cambridge University Press, 2007).

18. Thomas Hegghammer, *Jihad in Saudi Arabia: Violence and Pan-Islamism Since 1979* (Cambridge: Cambridge University Press, 2010).

19. In 2006, a diplomatic cable quoted a Saudi prince, who claims to speak for King Abdullah, as saying to Assistant to the U.S. President for Homeland Security and Counterterrorism Frances Townsend that in the event of war with Iran, Iran might use missiles against oil facilities, as well as attacks by both al-Qaeda and "the 'mini-Hizballah' in the Eastern Province." From Embassy Riyadh to Secretary of State, May 14, 2008, 08RIYADH768.

20. Ali Salman, interview with author, May 2011, Bahrain.

21. The unemployment program Hafiz, which was also announced by King Abdullah in Spring 2011 and started in late 2011, supports unemployed Saudis with two thousand riyals ($533) a month for up to a year, and has reportedly been paid to one million Saudis, after two million applied. "Hafiz: Inspiration for Job Seekers," *Arab News*, May 15, 2012, http://www.arabnews.com/saudi-arabia/hafiz-inspiration-job-seekers; David Ottaway, *Saudi Arabia's Race Against Time*, Wilson Center Middle East Program Occasional Paper Series, Summer 2012, http://www.wilsoncenter.org/publication/saudi-arabias-race-against-time-summer-2012, 5f.

22. "The Saudis Need Those High Oil Prices," *Bloomberg Businessweek*, February 23, 2012, http://www.businessweek.com/articles/2012-02-23/the-saudis-need-those-high-oil-prices. For the text of the royal decrees with the details of the spending programs, see www.spa.gov.sa/english/awamer.php.

23. While these announced handouts of wealth will benefit all Saudis, significant amounts went to government institutions from which the Shia are largely banned, such as the religious institutions and the security branches of the Interior Ministry.

24. "With $30 Billion Arms Deal, U.S. Bolsters Saudi Ties," *The New York Times*, December 29, 2011, http://www.nytimes.com/2011/12/30/world/middleeast/with-30-billion-arms-deal-united-states-bolsters-ties-to-saudi-arabia.html.

25. See Steffen Hertog, *Princes, Brokers, and Bureaucrats: Oil and the State in Saudi Arabia* (Ithaca, NY: Cornell University Press, 2010); Madawi al-Rasheed, "Circles of Power: Royals and

Saudi Society," in *Saudi Arabia in the Balance: Political Economy, Society, Foreign Affairs*, ed. Paul Aarts and Gerd Nonneman, 185–213 (London: Hurst, 2005).

26. Muhammad bin Nayef became interior minister on November 5, 2012, after a short interregnum by Ahmed bin Abd al-Aziz. Mitaab bin Abdullah, a son of King Abdullah, has been the commander of the Saudi National Guard since 2010, and Bandar bin Sultan was appointed director general of the main Saudi intelligence agency on July 19, 2012.

27. Sarah Yizraeli, *The Remaking of Saudi Arabia: The Struggle Between King Saud and Crown Prince Faysal, 1953–1962* (Tel Aviv: Dayan Center Papers, 1998).

28. "Al-Azhar Scholar Criticizes Saudi Edict Banning Protests," *Egypt Independent*, March 30, 2011, http://www.egyptindependent .com/news/al-azhar-scholar-criticizes-saudi-edict-banning-protests.

29. See Stéphane Lacroix, "Is Saudi Arabia Immune?" *Journal of Democracy* 22, no. 4 (October 2011): 48–59, at 56. The two main petitions were "*i'lan watani li-l-islah*" ["National Declaration for Reform"], *www.saudireform.com*; and "*nahwa dawlat al-huquq wa-l-mu'assasat*" ["Towards a State of Rights and Institutions"], www.dawlaty.com. The creators of both petitions maintained Twitter and Facebook accounts, where the text and the signatories are hosted. The petition from www.saudireform.com is available on http://www.facebook.com/note.php?note_id=191986637501121, and in an English translation at http://www.jadaliyya.com/pages/ index/753/a-call-from-saudi-intellectuals-to-the-political-l, and the petition on www.dawlaty.com is at https://www.facebook.com/ dawlaty.

30. Madawi Al-Rasheed, "No Saudi Spring: Anatomy of a Failed Revolution," *Boston Review*, March-April 2012. Al-Juhani was brought to trial in February 2012. Amnesty International, *Saudi Arabia: Trial of Riyadh Protester "Utterly Unwarranted"*, February 22, 2012, http://www.amnesty.org/en/news/saudi-arabia-trial -riyadh-protester-utterly-unwarranted-2012-02-22.

31. "Schüsse gegen Schiiten in Saudiarabien," *Neue Zürcher Zeitung*, March 12, 2011, http://www.nzz.ch/aktuell/startseite/schuesse -gegen-schiiten-in-saudiarabien-1.9860104; "Saudi Police Open Fire to Break Up a Protest," *The New York Times*, March 10, 2011, http:// www.nytimes.com/2011/03/11/world/middleeast/11saudi.html.

32. For more on the 2011–2012 transition in Yemen, see International Crisis Group, *Yemen: Enduring Conflicts, Threatened Transition*, July 3, 2012, http://www.crisisgroup.org/en/publication-type/ media-releases/2012/mena/yemen-enduring-conflicts-threatened -transition.aspx.

33. Tensions between the Houthis and *salafis* in Yemen have repeatedly escalated over the past years. Khaled Fattah, *Yemen's Sectarian Spring*, Sada, Carnegie Endowment for International Peace, May 11, 2012, https://www.carnegieendowment.org/sada/ 2012/05/11/yemen-s-sectarian-spring/apnv.

34. Keynote lecture given by Abdul Latif Al Zayani at the Gulf Research Meeting, University of Cambridge, July 11, 2012.

35. Author interview with a Bahraini economist, Bahrain, May 2011.

36. "al-'Utayshan: 18 miliyun musafir yu'abirun jisr al-malik fahd sanawiyyan" (al-'Utayshan: 18 Million Travellers Cross King Fahd Bridge Yearly," *Al-Hayat*, June 27, 2012, http://alhayat.com/ Details/413932.

37. According to eye witnesses in Bahrain, Saudi troops reportedly entered Bahrain during the height of the uprising in the 1990s, although that was not publicized. Author interviews, Bahrain, May 2011; and Kristian Coates Ulrichsen, "Bahrain: Evolution or Revolution?" *Open Democracy*, March 1, 2011, http://www.opendemocracy .net/kristian-coates-ulrichsen/bahrain-evolution-or-revolution.

38. Border guards checked IDs for Shia names and names of Shia villages and towns to determine if people were Shia. This practice started in late February 2011, before the crackdown. Various author interviews with Shia from the Eastern Province, 2011 and 2012.

39. The unity between the mainland oases of Qatif and al-Ahsa and the islands of Bahrain existed for most of the time between

the ninth and the fifteenth centuries, under different rulers such as the Qarmatians. The Qarmatians were a Sevener Shia Ismaili sect, and local historians argue that over the following centuries the bulk of the population switched to mainstream Twelver Shia beliefs. From the sixteenth century onward, when Bahrain came under Portuguese colonial rule and al-Ahsa was integrated into the Ottoman Empire, this political unity was destroyed but social, family, and religious links persisted. Historical writings produced by the Shia Islamist movements in the Gulf have depicted this period as the golden age of the Shia of Eastern Arabia, effectively formulating a *Bahrani* nativist historical myth. Louër, *Transnational*, 23, Matthiesen, *The Shia of Saudi Arabia*, 64–80.

40. The Al Khalifa do not personally follow the *Wahhabi* school of Sunni Islam, but rather the *maliki* school of Sunni religious law.

CHAPTER THREE

1. This defamation campaign was widely condemned. Bahrain Independent Commission of Inquiry, *Report of the Bahrain Independent Commission of Inquiry*, November 23, 2011, 389–401, www. bici.org.bh; Hasan Tariq al-Hasan, *On-Air, Online and On the Street: Understanding Bahrain's 2011 Counter-Revolution*, paper presented at the 3rd Gulf Research Meeting, University of Cambridge, July 11–14, 2012; Marc Owen Jones, "Social Media, Surveillance and Social Control in the Bahrain Uprising," *Westminster Papers in Communication and Culture* 10, no. 2 (April 2013): 71–91.

2. Toby Matthiesen, "Battling Over the Legacy of Bahrain's Pearl Roundabout," *Foreign Policy*, February 13, 2012, http://mideast .foreignpolicy.com/posts/2012/02/13/battling_over_the_legacy_ of_bahrain_s_pearl_roundabout.

3. Sectarian attacks against Shia have become widespread in Afghanistan and Pakistan. See, for example, "Pakistan Reels with Violence Against Shiites," *The New York Times*, December 3, 2012, http://www.nytimes.com/2012/12/04/world/asia/pakistans-hazara -shiites-under-siege.html.

4. www.alfateh.gov.bh/cms.php?task=Ahmed.

5. I visited some of the demolished mosques myself in May 2011. "While Bahrain Demolishes Mosques, U.S. Stays Silent," *McClatchy Newspapers*, May 8, 2011, http://www.mcclatchydc .com/2011/05/08/113839/while-bahrain-demolishes-mosques.html.

6. In September 2006 a report by Dr. Salah al-Bandar, a former adviser to the cabinet affairs minister, was published by the Gulf Centre for Democratic Development. Dubbed "Bandargate," it claimed to provide documentary evidence of a regime plan to marginalize Shia political actors and alter the country's sectarian makeup by naturalizing Sunni foreigners. The report is available online at www.bah rainrights.org/node/528. See also Laurence Louër, "The Political Impact of Labor Migration in Bahrain," *City & Society* (2008): 32–53.

7. "Citizenship as a Bahraini Government Tool," *Stratfor*, September 21, 2012, http://www.stratfor.com/sample/analysis/citizenship -bahraini-government-tool.

8. This is personified most famously in Ian Henderson, a colonial official who participated in the suppression of the Mau-Mau rebellion in Kenya in the 1950s and then went to Bahrain in 1964. There he remained in charge of Bahrain's internal security services long after formal independence in 1971 until 1998 and became infamous amongst the opposition for the brutal interrogation techniques he was said to have authorized. See Staci Strobl, "From Colonial Policing to Community Policing in Bahrain: The Historical Persistence of Sectarianism," *International Journal of Comparative and Applied Criminal Justice* 35, no. 1 (February 2011): 19–37; Kristian Coates Ulrichsen, "The Hollow Shell of Security Reform in Bahrain," *Foreign Policy*, April 12, 2012, http://mideast.foreignpolicy.com/posts/ 2012/04/12/the_hollow_shell_of_security_reform_in_bahrain.

9. "Bahrain Crown Prince Calls for Dialogue: TV," Reuters, February 18, 2011, http://www.reuters.com/article/2011/02/18/us -bahrain-crownprince-idUSTRE71H4OR20110218.

10. For details of the 2010 crackdown, see Christopher Davidson, *After the Sheikhs: The Coming Collapse of the Gulf Monarchies* (London: Hurst & Company, 2012), 141f.

11. He managed the popular discussion forum bahrainonline.org that was key in organizing protests over the last years, and particularly also the February 14 protests. See http://freeabdulemam.wordpress .com/2011/07/17/bahrain-leading-blogger-ali-abdulemam-sentenced -to-15-years-in-prison-along-with-other-human-rights-defenders.

12. Mansoor al-Jamri, interview with author, Bahrain, February 2011.

13. Muhammad Taqi al-Mudarrisi had been the leader of the political wing of the *shirazi* movement since its inception in the late 1960s in Iraq.

14. *Al-jabha al-islamiyya li tahrir al-Bahrayn.*

15. When Amal was banned in June 2012, this was partly justified by its following a cleric from abroad, Hadi al-Mudarrisi. "Bahrain: Group Follows Violent Shiite Cleric," *Gulf News*, June 5, 2012, http://gulfnews.com/news/gulf/bahrain/bahrain-group -follows-violent-shiite-cleric-1.1032052.

16. Rashid Hammada, '*asifa fawq miyah al-khalij: qissat awwal inqilab 'askari fi al-Bahrayn 1981 (A Storm on the Waters of the Gulf: Story of the First Military Coup in Bahrain 1981)* (London: Al-Safa lil-Nashr wa-l-Tawzi', 1990).

17. "Bahrainis Stripped of Citizenship," *al-Ahram Weekly*, November 21, 2012, http://weekly.ahram.org.eg/News/306/19/ Bahrainis-stripped-of-citizenship.aspx.

18. Author interview with a former member of the IFLB, London, 2010. A recent article by a Bahraini scholar who is the son of the chief of public security in Bahrain also tries to link the 1981 coup to Iran but fails to provide evidence to back up that claim. Hasan Tariq alHasan, "The Role of Iran in the Failed Coup of 1981: The IFLB in Bahrain," *The Middle East Journal*, 65, no. 4 (Autumn 2011): 603–617.

19. Author interview with Ahmad al-Shirazi, Kuwait, February 2012.

20. U.S. diplomatic cable released by Wikileaks: From Embassy Manama to Secretary of State, *Luncheon with King Hamad*, March 15, 2006, 06MANAMA409, http://wikileaks.org/cable/2006/03/ 06MANAMA409.html.

21. Author interview with a youth activist, Bahrain, May 2011.

22. Louër, *Transnational*, 83–88, 103–120; http://www.islam icdawaparty.com/?module=home&fname=history.php&active=7.

23. For an account of the Saudi branch of the Hizbullah networks, see Toby Matthiesen, "Hizbullah al-Hijaz: A History of the Most Radical Saudi Shi'a Opposition Group," *The Middle East Journal* 64, no. 2 (Spring 2010): 179–197.

24. Author interviews with cadres and supporters of al-Wifaq, Bahrain, February and May 2011.

25. Its Arabic name is *i'tilaf shabab thawrat 14 fibrayir*. Author online correspondence with a representative of the 14 February Coalition, April 2013. Its Facebook page, http://www.facebook. com/Coalition14th, has 61,505 likes and its Twitter page, @COALI TION14, has 61,738 followers as of March 27, 2013. A loose alliance of youths organized the initial February 14, 2011, demonstrations by summoning people to Manama's Pearl Roundabout via Facebook. One page called for a "day of rage," another for a "revolution" on February 14. See "thawrat 14 Fibrayir: al-ahdath al-yawmiyya (The 14 February Revolution: The Daily Events," *Bahrain Online*, February 25, 2011, http://bahrainonline.org/showthread.php?t=261420. See also Toby C. Jones and Ala'a Shehabi, "Bahrain's Revolutionaries," *Foreign Policy*, January 2, 2012, http://mideast.foreignpolicy .com/posts/2012/01/02/bahrains_revolutionaries.

26. Jane Kinninmont, *Bahrain: Beyond the Impasse*, Chatham House programme report, June 2012, http://www.chathamhouse .org/publications/papers/view/183983, 23; Author interview with a founder of the April 6 Youth Movement, Cairo, May 2013.

27. The Bahrain Youth Society for Human Rights was inspired by Otpor ("Resistance"), a non-partisan Serbian youth movement that, using non-violence, played a major role in the overthrow of Serbian president Slobodan Milošević in October 2000. In 2006, the society's founder, Muhammad al-Maskati, attended a training course with Otpor in Jordan, and the next year the society began issuing statements and reports on human rights and political opposition activities in Bahrain. Muhammad al-Maskati, interview

with author, Bahrain, May 2011. See also "Bullets Stall Youthful Push for Arab Spring," *The New York Times*, March 18, 2011, http://www.nytimes.com/2011/03/18/world/middleeast-/18youth.html; and the society's website at http://byshr.org.

28. In 1982, Said al-Shihabi and Mansoor al-Jamri founded the Bahrain Islamic Freedom Movement in London. While al-Jamri and others returned to Bahrain in 2001, al-Shihabi, dissatisfied with the 2002 constitution, remained in exile in London, from where he speaks on the group's behalf. See www.vob.org; Louër, *Transnational*, 28, 202; Sajjad Rizvi, "Shi'ism in Bahrain: Marja'iyya and Politics," *Orient*, no. 4 (2009): 16–24.

29. See "Bahraini "Coalition for a Republic" Issues First Statement," *Jadaliyya*, March 9, 2011, http://www.jadaliyya.com/pages/index/839/bahraini-coalition-for-a-republic-issues-first-sta.

30. "Hardline Shi'ite Groups Demand Republic in Bahrain," Reuters, March 8, 2011, http://af.reuters.com/article/worldNews/idAFTRE7272SU20110308.

31. Author online correspondence with a representative of the 14 February Coalition, April 2013.

32. For a detailed description of the dialogue, see Joost Hiltermann and Toby Matthiesen, "Bahrain Burning," *The New York Review of Books* (August 18, 2011), 49–51, http://www.nybooks.com/articles/archives/2011/aug/18/bahrain-burning; International Crisis Group, *Popular Protest in North Africa and the Middle East (VIII): Bahrain's Rocky Road to Reform*, July 28, 2011, 9–14, http://www.crisisgroup.org/en/regions/middle-east-north-africa/iraq-iran-gulf/bahrain/111-popular-protest-in-north-africa-and-the-middle-east-viii-bahrains-rocky-road-to-reform.aspx; Bahrain Independent Commission of Inquiry, 168f.

CHAPTER FOUR

1. "Bahrain Unrest: King Hamad Says Foreign Plot Foiled," BBC, March 21, 2011, http://www.bbc.co.uk/news/world-middle-east-12802945.

2. http://english.khamenei.ir/index.php?option=com_content &task=view&id=1581.

3. Created in 1986, it never constituted an integrated GCC army. Rather, units of national armies were at times formally assigned to the Peninsula Shield Force. This happened in March 2011, when Saudi Arabia and the UAE sent their national guard, army, and police units to Bahrain under the label Peninsula Shield Force. See Christian Koch, "The GCC as a Regional Security Organization," *Konrad Adenauer Stiftung International Reports* 11 (2010): 23–35.

4. Author interviews, Bahrain, February and May 2011. See Jane Kinninmont, *Bahrain: Beyond the Impasse*, Chatham House programme report, June 2012, http://www.chathamhouse.org/publica tions/papers/view/183983, 5f; Frederic Wehrey, "The March of Bahrain's Hardliners," Carnegie Middle East Center, May 2012, http:// carnegie-mec.org/publications/?fa=48299; *Bahrain Mirror*, February 17, 2012, http://bahrainmirror.com/article.php?id=3169&cid=74.

5. Marc Lynch, *The Arab Uprising: The Unfinished Revolutions of the New Middle East* (New York: PublicAffairs, 2012), 9. See also Toby Craig Jones, "Saudi Arabia Versus the Arab Spring," *Raritan: A Quarterly Review* 31, no. 2 (2011): 43–59. Gregory Gause III, on the other hand, argues that Saudi Arabia mainly acted counter-revolutionary in Bahrain, while it backed anti-regime forces in Libya and Syria and negotiated a transfer of power in Yemen. F. Gregory Gause III, *Saudi Arabia in the New Middle East*, Council on Foreign Relations Special Report, December 2011, http://www .cfr.org/saudi-arabia/saudi-arabia-new-middle-east/p26663.

6. Charles Tripp, *The Power and the People: Paths of Resistance in the Middle East* (Cambridge: Cambridge University Press, 2013), 110f.

7. Mona Kareem, "Bahrain: Mahazza Village Still Under Siege," *Global Voices*, December 10, 2012, http://globalvoicesonline.org/ 2012/12/10/bahrain-mahazza-village-still-under-siege.

8. For examples, see the Bahrain coverage of Reporters Without Borders and the list of people refused entry compiled by Bahrain Watch, at http://en.rsf.org/bahrain.html and bahrainwatch.org/access.

9. Some of the Shia in Bahrain, Kuwait, the UAE, Qatar, and Oman are of Iranian descent, while most Saudi Shia trace their lineage to Arab tribes from Najd or the local sedentary population in the Eastern Province.

10. The Bahrain Independent Commission of Inquiry attributes his death "to torture while in the custody of the NSA," the National Security Agency. Bahrain Independent Commission of Inquiry, *Report of the Bahrain Independent Commission of Inquiry*, November 23, 2011, 244f, www.bici.org.bh. See also Physicians for Human Rights, "Do No Harm: A Call for Bahrain to End Systematic Attacks on Doctors and Patients," April 2011, 24–25. The BICI report attributed thirteen civilian deaths to violence by the security forces in addition to five deaths attributed to torture. Bahrain Independent Commission of Inquiry, *Report*, 429f.

11. He was reinstated by the board of directors as editor-in-chief on August 4, 2011. Mansoor al-Jamri, e-mail conversation with author, January 2013.

12. "Torture in Bahrain Becomes Routine with Help from Nokia Siemens," *Bloomberg Markets Magazine*, August 22, 2011, http://www.bloomberg.com/news/2011-08-22/torture-in-bahrain -becomes-routine-with-help-from-nokia-siemens-networking.html.

13. The two former al-Wifaq MPs Jalal and Jawad Fairuz were among thirty-one Bahraini activists discussed in the previous chapter that were stripped of their citizenship in November 2012 for allegedly "breaching national security and damaging the supreme interests of the country." "Bahrainis Stripped of Citizenship," *al-Ahram Weekly*, November 21, 2012, http://weekly.ahram.org.eg/ News/306/19/Bahrainis-stripped-of-citizenship.aspx.

14. See http://freesharif.wordpress.com.

15. "Bahrain Court Upholds Life Sentences for Activists," Associated Press, September 4, 2012, http://www.guardian.co.uk/world/ feedarticle/10422048.

16. "Court in Bahrain Confirms Jail Terms for 13 Dissidents," *The New York Times*, January 7, 2013, www.nytimes.com/2013/01/ 08/world/middleeast/court-in-bahrain-confirms-jail-terms-for -13-dissidents.html.

17. Human Rights Watch, *Bahrain: Rights Activist Jailed for "Insulting" Tweets*, July 11, 2012, www.hrw.org/news/2012/07/11/bahrain-rights-activist-jailed-insulting-tweets. His initial sentence of three years was reduced to two upon appeal. "Activist's Conviction Upheld in Test of Pledges by Bahrain," *The New York Times*, December 11, 2012, www.nytimes.com/2012/12/12/world/middleeast/bahrain-court-upholds-activists-conviction.html.

18. Zainab al-Khawaja was arrested repeatedly in Bahrain throughout 2011, 2012, and 2013. See their Twitter accounts @MARYAMALKHAWAJA and @angryarabiya. See also Zainab's letter from prison announcing a hunger strike: Zainab al-Khawaja, "Why I Am on Hunger Strike in Bahrain," *The New York Times Blog*, March 24, 2013, http://kristof.blogs.nytimes.com/2013/03/24/a-letter-from-a-political-prisoner-on-hunger-strike-in-bahrain.

19. Author interview with a Bahraini opposition activist, Beirut, March 2013. See also *Bahrain Mirror*, January 2, 2012, http://www.bahrainmirror.com/article.php?id=2643&cid=117; and @Holy defince on Twitter.

20. Some of the protesters in Qatif, Saudi Arabia, tried to do the same, as exemplified by the Occupy Qatif twitter account, @OQatif. The self-description of this Twitter account, however, had more to do with *Bahrani* nativism than with the Global Occupy movement: "#Qatif, #Hasa, and #Awal (#Bahrain) will be united to become the historical Greater Bahrain." (Accessed on August 15, 2012).

21. "Disappearing Dissent: How Bahrain Buried Its Revolution," *Time*, November 29, 2011, http://world.time.com/2011/11/29/disappearing-dissent-how-bahrain-buried-its-revolution; "A Haven for Dissent in Bahrain, Where Lattes and Tear Gas Mix," *The New York Times*, December 28, 2011, www.nytimes.com/2011/12/29/world/middleeast/coffee-shop-clashes-show-how-bahrain-rules-fear-any-dissent.html.

22. In fact, in July 2012, Mahmud and his group, frustrated with the political stalemate in Bahrain and implicitly acknowledg-

ing that they had been used by the government against the protest movement, announced that henceforth they would try to operate independently of the government. Hasan Tariq Al Hasan, "'Too Big to Succeed': A Case of Sunni politics in Bahrain," *Open Democracy*, July 23, 2012, www.opendemocracy.net/hasan-tariq-al-hasan/%E2%80%98too-big-to-succeed%E2%80%99-case-of-sunni-politics-in-bahrain. For more on Sunni political mobilization, see Justin Gengler, "Bahrain's Sunni Awakening," *Middle East Report Online*, January 17, 2012, www.merip.org/mero/mero011712.

23. The Consultative Council is the upper house of the Bahraini National Assembly, which it forms together with the elected Council of Representatives. The Consultative Council usually represents royal interests, and can often block bills that the Council of Representatives wants to pass. The opposition wants to limit the powers of the Consultative Council, while the appointed members themselves think they are the ones who ensure stability. Author interviews with members of the Council of Representatives and the Consultative Council, May 2011, Bahrain.

24. The Muslim Brotherhood in Bahrain is formally organized in the Islamic National Forum (*al-minbar al-watani al-islami*). The main strands of Sunni Islamic politics to be found across the region have all long had a foothold in Bahrain. They include the Muslim Brotherhood, the *salafis*, and what could be called the Azhari strand, a group of scholars that had been educated at the al-Azhar University in Cairo but did not get involved with the two other major political groups. See 'Abbas Mirza al-Mirshid and 'Abd al-Hadi al-Khawaja, *al-tanzimat wa-l-jama'iyyat al-siyyasiyya fi al-Bahrayn* (*The Political Organizations and Groupings in Bahrain*) (Bahrain: Faradis lil-Nashr wa-l-Tawzi', 2008); Falah 'Abdallah al-Mudayris, *al-harakat wa-l-jama'at al-siyyasiyya fi al-Bahrayn 1937–2002* (*The Political Movements and Groups in Bahrain 1937–2002*) (Beirut: Dar al-Kunuz al-Adabiyya, 2004); and Baqir Salman al-Najjar, *al-harakat al-diniyya fi al-khalij al-'arabi* (*The Religious Movements in the Arabian Gulf*) (Beirut: Dar al-Saqi, 2007).

25. Another key slogan in both the Bahrain and Saudi Eastern Province protests is "*hayhat minna-l-dhilla*," a saying attributed to Imam Hussayn that loosely translates as "far away is the downtroddenness" or "no to humiliation."

26. International Crisis Group, *Popular Protest in North Africa and the Middle East (VIII): Bahrain's Rocky Road to Reform*, July 28, 2011, 18–20, http://www.crisisgroup.org/en/regions/middle-east -north-africa/iraq-iran-gulf/bahrain/111-popular-protest-in-north -africa-and-the-middle-east-viii-bahrains-rocky-road-to-reform. aspx. After pulling out of the dialogue, the opposition societies outlined their visions for the future and political demands for an elected government in the *Manama Document*, www.bahrainjdm .org/2011/10/13/manama-document-english.

27. "UPDATE 1-Fewer Than 1 in 5 Vote in Bahrain By-Elections," Reuters, September 25, 2011, http://www.reuters.com/article/2011/ 09/25/bahrain-vote-results-idUSL5E7KP13G20110925.

28. Geneive Abdo, "Talking About Reform in Bahrain," *Foreign Policy*, April 10, 2013, http://mideast.foreignpolicy.com/ posts/2013/04/10/talking_about_reform_in_bahrain.

29. Joost Hiltermann and Kelly McEvers, "Barricaded in Bahrain," *NYRBlog*, December 27, 2011, www.nybooks.com/blogs/ nyrblog/2011/dec/27/barricaded-bahrain.

30. See Bahrain Independent Commission of Inquiry, *Report*, 421.

31. Bahraini Information Affairs Authority, *BICI Follow-Up Report*, November 2012.

32. Bahrain Center for Human Rights, *The BICI Reforms: Promises of Progress, a Worsening Reality*, November 20, 2012, http://www .bahrainrights.org/en/node/5520.

33. Human Rights Watch, *Bahrain: Promises Unkept, Rights Still Violated, Head of Independent Commission: Implementation "Inadequate*," November 22, 2012, http://www.hrw.org/news/2012/11/22/ bahrain-promises-unkept-rights-still-violated.

34. The other was John Timoney, the former Miami police chief, who was criticized for his heavy-handed policing of demon-

strations. Kristian Coates Ulrichsen, "The Hollow Shell of Security Reform in Bahrain," *Foreign Policy*, April 12, 2012, http://mideast .foreignpolicy.com/posts/2012/04/12/the_hollow_shell_of_security _reform_in_bahrain.

35. See PR Watch, http://bahrainwatch.org/pr.

36. Physicians for Human Rights, *Weaponizing Tear Gas, Bahrain's Unprecedented Use of Toxic Chemical Agents Against Civilians*, http:// physiciansforhumanrights.org/library/reports/weaponizing-tear-gas .html, August 2012.

37. Lulua TV. *Lulua* is the Arabic word for *Pearl*.

CHAPTER FIVE

1. Translation by MEMRI, www.youtube.com/watch?v=Nb -OSh5Hnvw.

2. "Security Source Comments on a Politicized Friday Sermon by a Qatif-Based Sheikh," *Saudi Press Agency* and *al-Riyyad* newspaper, February 20, 2012, www.alriyadh.com:8080/en/article/711953.

3. This information stems from over one hundred author interviews with Saudi Shia and Saudi officials during two field trips to Saudi Arabia, in 2008 and 2011. For sources and citations on the protest movement in Eastern Saudi Arabia, see Toby Matthiesen, "A 'Saudi Spring?': The Shi'a Protest Movement in the Eastern Province 2011–2012," *The Middle East Journal* 66, no. 4 (Autumn 2012): 628–659. See also 'Abd al-Rahman Muhammad 'Umar al-'Uqayl, *ahdath al-'Awwamiyya wa-l-Qatif* (*The Events of Awwamiyya and Qatif: From 10 February 2011 to 10 February 2012*) (2012), https://www.awamia.net/index.php/permalink/5991.html.

4. For a powerful dispelling of the myth of the reformist king, see Andrew Hammond, *The Islamic Utopia: The Illusion of Reform in Saudi Arabia* (London: Pluto Press, 2012), 117–153.

5. In many ways this is similar to Bahrain, where the opposition came home from exile when the new King Hamad took over the throne but failed to keep his promises of genuine democratic reform. The opposition then split over whether to participate in

parliamentary elections and whether to negotiate with the regime after the 2011 uprising.

6. Toby Matthiesen, *Diwaniyyas, Intellectual Salons and the Limits of Civil Society in Saudi Arabia*, Middle East Institute, October 2009, http://www.mei.edu/content/diwaniyyas-intellectual-salons-and-limits-civil-society, 13–15.

7. Nimr al-Nimr blamed the Saudi leadership for the events in Medina and for the situation of the Shia in general, before concluding that "our dignity is more precious than the unity of the land and the unity of the *umma* and if we don't get our dignity in a different way we will not shy away from secession." This and other, similarly harsh statements caused outrage amongst other Saudis, but gained him the support of many Saudi Shia youth. For a discussion of the 2009 events, see Toby Matthiesen, "The Shi'a of Saudi Arabia at a Crossroads," *Middle East Report Online*, May 6, 2009, http://www.merip.org/mero/mero050609; Human Rights Watch, *Saudi Arabia: Denied Dignity Systematic Discrimination and Hostility Toward Saudi Shia Citizens*, 2009, http://www.hrw.org/node/85348, 15–21. See also U.S. diplomatic cable released by Wikileaks: From Embassy Riyadh to Secretary of State, *Meeting with Controversial Shi'a Sheikh Nimr Al-Nimr*, August 23, 2008, 08Riyadh1283, http://wikileaks.org/cable/2008/08/08RIYADH1283.html.

8. F. Gregory Gause III, *The International Relations of the Persian Gulf* (Cambridge: Cambridge University Press, 2010), 128–132; Toby Matthiesen, "Hizbullah al-Hijaz: A History of the Most Radical Saudi Shi'a Opposition Group," *The Middle East Journal* 64, no. 2 (Spring 2010): 179–197.

9. See Matthiesen, "A 'Saudi Spring'?" 645f.

10. "MOI's Official Source: Number of Security Checks, Vehicles Coming Under Gunfire Attacks by Assailants in Qatif," *Saudi Press Agency*, November 24, 2011, http://www.spa.gov.sa/English/print.php?id=946403.

11. "4 Killed in Exchange of Gunfire in Qatif: MOI," *Saudi Gazette*, November 24, 2011, www.saudigazette.com.sa/index.cfm?method=home.regcon&contentID=20111125112725.

12. In May 2012, two men were jailed in this corruption scam, and new flood prevention projects were promised. "Saudi Arabia to Punish Officials for Damage After Jeddah Floods," *Bloomberg*, February 2, 2011, http://www.bloomberg.com/news/2011-02-02/saudi-arabia-to-punish-officials-for-damage-after-jeddah-floods.html; "Long-Term Jeddah Flood Projects Will Be Ready by September 2013," *Arab News*, July 19, 2012, http://www.arabnews.com/long-term-jeddah-flood-projects-will-be-ready-september-2013; "Two Jailed Over Jeddah Floods Corruption," *Arabian Business*, May 30, 2012, http://www.arabianbusiness.com/two-jailed-over-jeddah-floods-corruption-459882.html.

13. For information on this protest campaign, see @e3teqal on Twitter, and "Saudis Stage Rare Protest Over Security Detentions Without Trial," Reuters, September 10, 2012, http://english.ahram.org.eg/News/52465.aspx. See also Stéphane Lacroix, "Is Saudi Arabia Immune?" *Journal of Democracy* 22, no. 4 (October 2011): 48–59.

14. Amnesty International, *Saudi Arabia: 11 Women Still Held After Protest*, January 8, 2013, http://www.amnesty.org/en/news/saudi-arabia-release-11-women-held-after-peaceful-protest-2013-01-08.

15. "161 Arrested in Buraidah," *Arab News*, March 2, 2013, http://www.arabnews.com/saudi-arabia/161-arrested-buraidah.

16. "Prominent Saudi Activists Sentenced to Jail," *Riyadh Bureau*, March 9, 2013, http://riyadhbureau.com/blog/2013/3/acpra-sentence. See also their website at http://www.acpra-hr.co; and Nora Abdulkarim, "Trial of Saudi Civil Rights Activists Mohammad al-Qahtani and Abdullah al-Hamid," *Jadaliyya*, September 3, 2012, www.jadaliyya.com/pages/index/7174/trial-of-saudi-civil-rights-activists-mohammad-al-.

17. All of these campaigns relied heavily on social media for propaganda, interregional organization, and international publicity. Nitin Agarwal, Merlyna Lim, and Rolf T. Wigand, "Online Collective Action and the Role of Social Media in Mobilizing Opinions: A Case Study on Women's Right-to-Drive Campaigns in Saudi Arabia," in *Web 2.0 Technologies and Democratic Governance: Political, Policy and Management Implications*, ed. Christopher G. Reddick and Stephen K. Aikins, 99–123 (New York: Springer, 2012).

18. Hugh Eakin, "Will Saudi Arabia Ever Change?" *The New York Review of Books*, December 12, 2012, http://www.nybooks .com/articles/archives/2013/jan/10/will-saudi-arabia-ever-change; "Saudi Women on Shura Council," *al-Ahram Weekly*, January 16, 2013, http://weekly.ahram.org.eg/News/1037/19/Saudi-women -on-Shura-Council.aspx.

19. "Clerics Protest Outside the Royal Court," *Riyadh Bureau*, January 15, 2013, http://riyadhbureau.com/blog/2013/1/clerics-protest -royal-court.

20. The letter was released on his Twitter account, @salman_ alodah, where he has over 2.5 million followers as of April 2013.

21. Author interview with a campaign aide, December 2011, al-Ahsa; "Empty Voting Booths Signal Little Enthusiasm at Rare Saudi Polls," *The Daily Star*, September 30, 2011, http://www.dailystar.com .lb/News/Middle-East/2011/Sep-30/150058-empty-voting-booths -signal-little-enthusiasm-at-rare-saudi-polls.ashx#axzz2QS4modeS.

22. Saudi Press Agency, English Website, October 4, 2011, www .spa.gov.sa/English/details.php?id=931281.

23. Toby Matthiesen, "Saudi Arabia: The Middle East's Most Under-Reported Conflict," *Guardian.co.uk*, January 23, 2011, www .guardian.co.uk/commentisfree/2012/jan/23/saudi-arabia-shia -protesters.

24. "Security Source Comments on a Politicized Friday Sermon by a Qatif-Based Sheikh."

25. The idea that protest movements develop protest cycles or cycles of contention draws upon the work of Sidney Tarrow. See Sidney Tarrow, *Power in Movement: Social Movements and Contentious Politics*, 2nd. ed. (Cambridge: Cambridge University Press, 1998), 141–160. For an application of this notion to the 1990s uprising in Bahrain, see Fred H. Lawson, "Repertoires of Contention in Contemporary Bahrain," in *Islamic Activism: A Social Movement Theory Approach*, ed. Quintan Wiktorowicz (Bloomington, IN: Indiana University Press, 2004), 89–111.

26. Toby Matthiesen, "Saudi Arabia's Shiite Escalation," *Foreign Policy*, July 10, 2012, http://mideast.foreignpolicy.com/posts/2012/ 07/10/sable_rattling_in_the_gulf.

27. While the different political groups in Qatif maintained their online activism, some started to cooperate more closely through the formal structure of the Coalition for Freedom and Justice (*i'tilaf al-hurriyya wa-l-'adala*), announced on March 25, 2012. Author Skype interview with a youth activist from Qatif, September 2012. Rosie Bsheer, "Saudi Revolutionaries: An Interview," *Jadaliyya*, June 21, 2012, http://www.jadaliyya.com/pages/index/6104/saudi-revolutionaries_an-interview. See the Facebook page of the coalition at http://www.facebook.com/cofaj.

28. "Two Killed as Saudi Security Forces Try to Arrest Shi'ite Man," Reuters, September 27, 2012, http://www.reuters.com/article/2012/09/27/us-saudi-shiite-deaths-idUSBRE88Q0LM20120927, "Shiite Dies of Wounds After Saudi Police Raid Family," Agence France-Presse, September 29, 2012, http://www.google.com/hostednews/afp/article/ALeqM5i7kD6bs1FX_xEBCsO9cv5hJQQWrg?docId=CNG.f4d4fec426309741ec996fb87c31f219.14c1.

29. "Man Shot Dead as Police Clash with Shi'ites in Saudi Arabia," Reuters, December 28, 2012, www.reuters.com/article/2012/12/28/us-saudi-shiite-shooting-idUSBRE8BR05J20121228.

30. Muhammad bin Fahd had been governor of the Eastern Province since 1985. For those sympathetic to the protests Muhammad bin Fahd was cracking down too harshly on the protestors. For hardliners in the Saudi ruling family, on the other hand, he was probably not ruthless enough. Toby Matthiesen, "Saudi Royal Family Politics and the Arab Spring," *Foreign Policy*, January 14, 2013, http://mideast.foreignpolicy.com/posts/2013/01/14/saudi_royal_family_politics_and_the_arab_spring.

31. "Saudi Says Detained 'Spy Ring' Linked to Iran," aljazeera .com, March 26, 2013, http://www.aljazeera.com/news/middleeast/2013/03/2013326181050797572.html.

32. Author e-mail correspondence with several of the signatories, April 2013.

1. Kristian Coates Ulrichsen, "Kuwait: Political Crisis at Critical Juncture," BBC, October 23, 2012, www.bbc.co.uk/news/world-middle-east-20026581.

2. "Amir Orders Change to Election Law," *Arab Times*, October 19, 2012, http://www.arabtimesonline.com/NewsDetails/tabid/96/smid/414/ArticleID/189124/reftab/36/t/Amir-orders-change-to-election-law/Default.aspx.

3. Mary Ann Tétreault, *Stories of Democracy: Politics and Society in Contemporary Kuwait* (New York: Columbia University Press, 2000), 44–48. This division goes back to Ibn Khaldūn's historical sociology of Arab societies, in which the main characteristic of Arab history is the *badu-hadar* dichotomy. Ibn Khaldūn, *The Muqaddimah: An Introduction to History*, trans. Franz Rosenthal, ed. N. J. Dawood (Princeton, NJ: Princeton University Press, 1967).

4. @KarametWatan.

5. There are no official figures for the number of Shia in Kuwait. A U.S. diplomatic cable released by Wikileaks states that 30 percent of Kuwaiti citizens are Shia. From Embassy Kuwait to Secretary of State, *Kuwait's Stateless Bidoon: Background and Recent Promising Developments*, June 3, 2009, 09KUWAIT558, http://wikileaks.org/cable/2009/06/09KUWAIT558.html. See also Rivka Azoulay, "The Politics of Shi'i Merchants in Kuwait," in *Business Politics in the Middle East*, ed. Steffen Hertog, Giacomo Luciani, Marc Valeri, 67–99 (London: Hurst, 2013), 72.

6. Most Hasawis, whose name indicates they originally hail from the al-Ahsa or Hasa oasis, adhere to an esoteric strand of Shiism, the *shaykhiyya*, which follows the teachings of Shia cleric Ahmad al-Ahsai (1753–1826). The *shaykhiyya* is relatively strong both in Kuwait and the al-Ahsa province of Saudi Arabia, but its clerics and leading notables tend to avoid confronting the Gulf ruling families, which sometimes puts them at odds with their more politically minded Shia counterparts. Author interviews with leaders from both the Kuwaiti and the Saudi Shaikhi community, Kuwait, February 2012.

7. Author interview with a Shia activist, Kuwait, February 2012. Two Shia MPs received death threats over their support of the Bahraini protests and their support for the Syrian regime. Mona Kareem, "Shiaphobia Hits Kuwait," *Jadaliyya*, May 17, 2011, www.jadaliyya .com/pages/index/1603/shiaphobia-hits-kuwait.

8. "Bahrain Denies Kuwaiti Role in Dialogue," *Gulf Daily News*, March 29, 2011, http://www.gulf-daily-news.com/NewsDetails .aspx?storyid=302772; "Bahrain Shuns Kuwait's Mediation Offer," aljazeera.com, March 28, 2011, http://www.aljazeera.com/NEWS/ MIDDLEEAST/2011/03/201132811747469782.html.

9. Author interviews with Shia activists, Kuwait, February 2012. Kareem, "Shiaphobia Hits Kuwait."

10. "Kuwait Naval Units Join Bahrain Mission . . . 'Plot Foiled'," *Arab Times*, March 21, 2011, www.arabtimesonline.com/NewsDetails/ tabid/96/smid/414/ArticleID/167038/reftab/116/Default.aspx.

11. "MPs Press to Arm Syrian Opposition: Kuwait Urged to Cut Ties with Damascus," *Arab Times*, March 1, 2012, http://www .arabtimesonline.com/NewsDetails/tabid/96/smid/414/ArticleID/ 180241/reftab/96/t/MPs-press-to-arm-Syrian-opposition/Default .aspx.

12. Gwenn Okruhlik, "The Identity Politics of Kuwait's Election," *Foreign Policy*, February 8, 2012, http://mideast.foreignpolicy .com/posts/2012/02/08/the_identity_politics_of_kuwait_s_election.

13. It is called the Islamic Constitutional Movement (*al-haraka al-dusturiyya al-islamiyya: Hadas*). Nathan J. Brown, "Pushing Toward Party Politics? Kuwait's Islamic Constitutional Movement," Carnegie Endowment for International Peace, February 2007, http://carnegieendowment.org/2007/02/13/pushing-toward -party-politics-kuwait-s-islamic-constitutional-movement/3kex.

14. The Shia channels operated by the *shirazis* include al-Anwar, al-Anwar II, al-Mahdi, and CH 4 Teen. The Kuwait branch of the Hizbullah networks is said to operate the al-Kut channel. Author interviews with Shia journalists, Kuwait, February 2012.

15. Marc Lynch, *The Arab Uprising: The Unfinished Revolutions of the New Middle East* (New York: PublicAffairs, 2012), 139f.

16. *Al-Dar* was financed by the Shia businessman Mahmud Haydar. Abd al-Hussayn al-Sultan, former editor-in-chief of al-Dar newspaper, interview with author, Kuwait, February 2012.

17. In Spring 2012, the trial of Hamad al-Naqi (@alnaqiq8) for these Twitter comments galvanized feelings across the region, symbolizing how important both social media and sectarianism had become. "Kuwaiti Gets 10 Years for Twitter Blasphemy: Lawyer," Reuters, June 4, 2012, http://www.reuters.com/article/2012/06/04/us-kuwait-prophet-verdict-idUSBRE8530DK20120604; Human Rights Watch, *Kuwait: 10 Years for Criticizing Neighboring Rulers: Emir Vetoes Legislation Authorizing Death for "Mocking Religion,"* press release, June 7, 2012, http://www.hrw.org/news/2012/06/07/kuwait-10-years-criticizing-neighboring-rulers.

18. The Interior Ministry had unsuccessfully tried to ban him from running in the February 2012 elections. He was also elected in the December 2012 elections. "Court Reinstates Kuwaiti Parliamentary Candidates," *Gulf News*, January 20, 2012, http://gulfnews.com/news/gulf/kuwait/court-reinstates-kuwaiti-parliamentary-candidates-1.968562.

19. 'Abd al-Hamid 'Abbas Dashti, *tarikh shi'at al-khalij wa 'aqa'idhum* (*The History of Shia in the Gulf and Their Beliefs*) (n.p.: Dar Zaynas lil-Nashr wa-l-'Ilam, 2008).

20. Abd al-Hamid Dashti, interview with author, Kuwait, February 2012. For a video of one such event, see http://www.youtube.com/watch?v=r17qgtiy0Z4.

21. Azoulay, "The Politics of Shi'i Merchants in Kuwait," 71–77.

22. For more on Kuwaiti Shia see 'Abd al-Muhsin Yusuf Jamal, *lamahat min tarikh al-shi'a fi al-Kuwayt (al-fitra min nasha'at al-Kuwayt ila al-istiqlal)* (*Glances from the History of the Shia in Kuwait: The Era from the Establishment of Kuwait to Independence*) (Kuwait: Dar al-Naba' lil-Nashr, 2005); Laurence Louër, *Transnational Shiite Politics: Religious and Political Networks in the Gulf* (New York: Columbia University Press, 2008), 46–57, 167–176; Falah 'Abdallah al-Mudayris, *al-haraka al-shi'iyya fi al-Kuwayt* (*The Shia Movement in Kuwait*) (Kuwait: Dar al-Qurtas, 1999).

23. See Lori Plotkin Boghardt, *Kuwait Amid War, Peace and Revolution: 1979–1991 and New Challenges* (Basingstoke: Palgrave Macmillan, 2006).

24. For background on the various Islamist groups in Kuwait, see Falah Abdullah al-Mdaires, *Islamic Extremism in Kuwait: From the Muslim Brotherhood to Al-Qaeda and other Islamic Political Groups* (London: Routledge, 2010).

25. They were Adnan Abd al-Samad and Ahmad Lari from the National Islamic Alliance (*al-tahaluf al-watani al-islami*). The alliance, which locally is known as the Kuwaiti branch of the Hizbullah networks, gained five seats in the December 2012 elections, making it the strongest political force amongst the Shia of Kuwait. See the Kuwait Politics Database at Georgia State University, http://www2.gsu.edu/~polmfh/database/database.htm.

26. Two security officers were killed in that operation. "Kuwait MPs Decry Rally for "Terrorist" Mughniyah," *Al Arabiya News*, February 17, 2008, http://www.alarabiya.net/articles/2008/02/17/45771.html; "Kuwait MPs Expelled for Mourning Mughniyah," *Al Arabiya News*, February 20, 2008, http://www.alarabiya.net/articles/2008/02/20/45901.html.

27. "Kuwait MPs Expelled for Mourning Mughniyah." The Popular Action Bloc (*kutlat al-'amal al-sha'bi*) was founded by veteran MP Ahmad al-Saadun and was made up of seven opposition MPs, including Musallam al-Barrak, who in 2012 would emerge as the figurehead of the protest movement.

28. Ghanim al-Najjar, professor of political science at Kuwait University, interview with author, December 2012.

29. The mobilization in 2006 was facilitated by mobile phones and the Internet, and it politicized a whole generation of youth. Mary Ann Tétreault, "Kuwait's Annus Mirabilis," *Merip Online*, September 7, 2006, www.merip.org/mero/mero090706.

30. Author interview with a leader of the youth movement, Kuwait, December 2012. The slogan was popularized on this blog: www.altariq2009.com.

31. Kuwaiti youth movements have often formed as ad-hoc coalitions around specific goals. Kristin Diwan, "Kuwait's Impatient Youth Movement," *Foreign Policy*, June 29, 2011, http://mideast.foreignpolicy.com/posts/2011/06/29/kuwait_s_youth_movement.

32. Mainly of the three most populous tribes in Kuwait: al-'Awazim, al-'Ajman, and al-Mutran.

33. The Civil Democratic Movement (*al-haraka al-dimuqratiyya al-madaniyya*) has bylaws, internal elections, and a formal structure, which is a novelty for Kuwaiti youth groups. Author interview with a leader of the Civil Democratic Movement, Kuwait, December 2012. http://www.cdmkw.com.

34. Kristian Coates Ulrichsen, "Kuwait: Kuwait's Black Monday," *The World Today* 67, no. 12 (December 2011); "Kuwait's Prime Minister Resigns After Protests," BBC, November 28, 2011, http://www.bbc.co.uk/news/world-middle-east-15931526.

35. Author interview with a leader of the youth movement, Kuwait, December 2012. See also "Youth Movement Helps to Set Kuwait's Political Agenda," *The National*, July 22, 2012, www.thenational.ae/news/world/middle-east/youth-movement-helps-to-set-kuwait-s-political-agenda; "Kuwaiti Youth Emerge as Force in Protests Against the State," *Al-Monitor*, translated from *al-Hayat*, October 22, 2012, http://www.al-monitor.com/pulse/politics/2012/10/kuwaiti-youth-look-forward-to-new-political-epoch.html.

36. Author interview with a former MP and member of the majority bloc, Kuwait, December 2012.

37. "Kuwait Protest at Court Ruling Dissolving Parliament," BBC, June 27, 2012, www.bbc.co.uk/news/world-middle-east-18606540.

38. The parliament can express no confidence in ministers, including the prime minister, and draft laws, even though they have to be approved by the amir. Cabinet ministers, including the prime minister, are automatically granted membership in the Assembly, effectively increasing the number of MPs from fifty to sixty-six. The appointed ministers often vote in the interests of the ruling family.

39. Tétreault, *Stories of Democracy*.

40. "In Bid to End Crisis, Kuwait's Parliament Is Dissolved," *The New York Times*, October 7, 2012, www.nytimes.com/2012/10/08/world/middleeast/in-bid-to-end-crisis-kuwaits-parliament-is-dissolved.html.

41. Kristin Smith Diwan, "Kuwait's Balancing Act," *Foreign Policy*, October 23, 2012, http://mideast.foreignpolicy.com/posts/2012/10/23/kuwait_s_balancing_act.

42. Reflecting divisions between different branches of the ruling family, as well as generational divisions, some, particularly younger members, of the al-Sabah family are sympathetic to the protest movement, and two were also briefly arrested for posting pro-opposition tweets. "Kuwait Releases Royals Detained Over Tweets," aljazeera.com, November 10, 2012, http://www.aljazeera.com/news/middleeast/2012/11/2012111014411070590707.html.

43. "Kuwait Emir's Change to Election Rules Stirs Signs of Arab Spring," *The Guardian*, November 25, 2012, http://www.guardian.co.uk/world/2012/nov/25/kuwait-elections-unrest-emir-change-voting-rules.

44. "Kuwait: Ex-MP Mussallam al-Barrak Freed on Bail," BBC, November 1, 2012, http://www.bbc.co.uk/news/world-middle-east-20165318. For a timeline of protests, see Mary Ann Tétreault, "Looking for Revolution in Kuwait," *Merip Online*, November 1, 2012, www.merip.org/mero/mero110112.

45. "Kuwait Election: Thousands Join Anti-Government Protest," BBC, November 30, 2012, http://www.bbc.co.uk/news/world-middle-east-20558819.

46. The opposition claims it was lower, around 30 percent. Author interview with a former MP and member of the majority bloc, Kuwait, December 2012.

47. "Shiites Score Big in Kuwaiti Poll Hit by Boycott," *Ahram Online*, December 2, 2012, http://english.ahram.org.eg/News/59602.aspx. In the February 2012 elections there were only seven Shia MPs. The December 2012 parliament also included a relatively

high number of women. Kuwait Politics Database at Georgia State University.

48. "The Price of Kuwait's Election Boycott," *Deutsche Welle*, December 3, 2012, http://www.dw.de/the-price-of-kuwaits-election -boycott/a-16423752.

49. Author interview with Jawad Bukhamseen, a prominent Shia businessman, Kuwait, February 2012.

50. This was Dignity of a Nation rally number 4. "Kuwaiti Protesters Rally to Scrap New Parliament," Agence France-Presse, December 8, 2012, http://english.ahram.org.eg/NewsContent/2/8/60067/World/ Region/Kuwaiti-protesters-rally-for-scrapping-new-parliam.aspx.

51. Another Dignity of a Nation rally was held on January 22, 2013 (number 7).

52. Author interview with a founder of the opposition coalition, Kuwait, March 2013. See the Twitter account of the Popular Action Movement (*harakat al-'amal al-sha'bi*) @7ashd.

53. "Kuwait Court to Consider Al Barrak's Appeal on Monday," *Gulf News*, April 18, 2013, http://gulfnews.com/news/gulf/kuwait/ kuwait-court-to-consider-al-barrak-s-appeal-on-monday-1.1172187.

54. This is the figure quoted in a U.S. diplomatic cable released by Wikileaks. From Embassy Kuwait to Secretary of State, *Kuwait's Stateless Bidoon: Background and Recent Promising Developments*, June 3, 2009, 09KUWAIT558, http://wikileaks.org/cable/2009/ 06/09KUWAIT558.html. An unknown number of stateless people live in other states of the Gulf, particularly in the UAE and Saudi Arabia. Christopher Davidson, *After the Sheikhs: The Coming Collapse of the Gulf Monarchies* (London: Hurst & Company, 2012), 134–139.

55. For more on the *Bidun*, see Human Rights Watch, *Prisoners of the Past: Kuwaiti Bidun and the Burden of Statelessness*, June 13, 2011, http://www.hrw.org/reports/2011/06/13/prisoners-past-0; and Claire Beaugrand, "Statelessness & Administrative Violence: *Bidūns'* Survival Strategies in Kuwait," *The Muslim World* 101 (2011): 228–250.

56. Author interview with a former MP and member of the majority bloc, Kuwait, December 2012.

57. While the majority of the Shia *Bidun* follow as their *marji'* *al-taqlid* Ali al-Sistani, many also follow Sadiq al-Shirazi as well as Ali Khamenei. Author interview with a *Bidun* rights activist, Kuwait, December 2012.

58. For details on the *Bidun* protests, see www.bedoonrights .org.

59. While the government announced in March 2013 that "4,000 foreigners," a way to avoid referring to the *Bidun* as stateless citizens, would be given citizenship, this did not solve the fundamental problem of the *Bidun*. Mona Kareem, "Is Kuwait Serious About Bedoon Naturalization?" *Al-Monitor*, March 27, 2013, http://www.al-monitor.com/pulse/originals/2013/03/kuwait -bedoon-naturalization.html.

60. Jane Kinninmont, *Kuwait's Parliament: An Experiment in Semi-Democracy*, Chatham House briefing paper, August 2012, http://www.chathamhouse.org/publications/papers/view/185357. See also Greg Power, *The Difficult Development of Parliamentary Politics in the Gulf: Parliaments and the Process of Managed Reform in Kuwait, Bahrain and Oman*, London School of Economics, Kuwait Research Programme, October 2012, http://www2.lse.ac.uk/government/ research/resgroups/kuwait/research/projects/parliaments.aspx.

CHAPTER SEVEN

1. This slogan makes reference to the notion of Ancient Bahrain. Protesters shout "Death to the oppressors,' but without directly mentioning the Al Khalifa. See videos uploaded by *oman-protests* on Youtube and "Omani's Staged Protest to Condemn Killing of Oppressed Bahraini's," March 19, 2011, http://www.youtube .com/watch?v=3xHVeVlWfbU&feature=plcp.

2. "Elsewhere in the Arabian Gulf: A Peaceful Anti-Corruption Protest in Oman," *Slate*, February 18, 2011, http://www.slate.com/ articles/news_and_politics/dispatches/2011/02/elsewhere_in_the_ arabian_gulf.html.

3. The Arabic original can be found here: http://www.youtube.com/watch?v=Bm_AxeWKgpA. An English translation is at www.democracynow.org/2012/12/7/qatari_human_rights_official_defends_life.

4. Author interviews with officials and parliamentarians in Oman and Kuwait, February and March 2013.

5. See, for example, this case from Kuwait: "Kuwait Lengthens Sentence of Man who 'Insulted' Emir: Lawyer," *The Daily Star*, March 21, 2013, http://m.dailystar.com.lb/News/Middle-East/2013/Mar-21/211026-kuwait-lengthens-sentence-of-man-who-insulted-emir-lawyer.ashx; and Jane Kinninmont, "To What Extent Is Twitter Changing Gulf Societies?" Chatham House, February 2012, http://www.chathamhouse.org/sites/default/files/public/Research/Middle%20East/0213kinninmont.pdf.

6. Ra'id Zuhair Al-Jamali, "Oman, Kind of Not Quiet?" *Foreign Policy*, November 7, 2011, http://mideast.foreignpolicy.com/posts/2011/11/07/kind_of_not_quiet; James Worrall, "Oman: The 'Forgotten' Corner of the Arab Spring," *Middle East Policy* 19, no. 3 (Fall 2012): 98–115.

7. Author interview with a protester, Sohar, Oman, February 2013.

8. Marc Valeri, *The Qaboos-State Under the Test of the "Omani Spring": Are the Regime's Answers Up to Expectations?*, http://www.sciencespo.fr/ceri/sites/sciencespo.fr.ceri/files/art_mv.pdf; "Oman Protests Spread, Road to Port Blocked," Reuters, February 28, 2011, http://www.reuters.com/article/2011/02/28/us-oman-protests-idUSTRE71Q0U420110228.

9. Said Sultan al Hashimi, *The Omani Spring: Towards the Break of a New Dawn*, Arab Reform Initiative, November 2011, http://www.arab-reform.net/omani-spring-towards-break-new-dawn.

10. Author interview with a member of the Majlis al-Shura, February 2013.

11. Author interviews with activists in Sohar and Muscat, Oman, February 2013.

12. Marc Valeri, "'Qaboos Can Make Mistakes Like Anybody Else'— The Sultan of Oman De-Sacralized," *Jadaliyya*, November 18, 2012, http://www.jadaliyya.com/pages/index/8430/%E2%80%9Cqaboos-can-make-mistakes-like-anybody-else_-the-s.

13. For an account of the early formation of the *Ibadiyya*, see John C. Wilkinson, *Ibadism: Origins and Early Development in Oman* (Oxford: Oxford University Press, 2010).

14. The *Lawatiyya* largely migrated from India between the mid-eighteenth century and the end of the nineteenth century. Author interviews with *Lawatis*, Muscat, Oman, February 2013; Marc Valeri, "High Visibility, Low Profile: The Shi'a in Oman under Sultan Qaboos," *International Journal of Middle East Studies* 42, no. 2 (2010): 251–268: 259f, 263f.

15. Protesters in early 2011 specifically asked for the removal of Maqbool bin Ali bin Sultan, as they accused him of corruption, and he was replaced in late February 2011 and became minister of transport and communications. After just one week, he was fired from that position, too, and not given any other official position. Marc Valeri, e-mail correspondence with author, January 2013; "Sultan Qaboos Reshuffles Oman Cabinet," *Gulf News*, February 26, 2011, http://gulfnews.com/news/gulf/oman/sultan-qaboos-reshuffles-oman-cabinet-1.768277.

16. "Omani's Staged Protest to Condemn Killing of Oppressed Bahraini's," March 19, 2011, http://www.youtube.com/watch?v=3xHVeVlWfbU&feature=plcp.

17. Author interview with an Omani Shia intellectual, London, 2012.

18. Marc Valeri, "Identity Politics and Nation-Building under Sultan Qaboos," in *Sectarian Politics in the Gulf*, ed. Lawrence G. Potter (London: Hurst, forthcoming).

19. "Oman Protests Suggest Jobs, Reform Pledges Fall Short," Reuters, July 4, 2012, http://www.reuters.com/article/2012/07/04/us-oman-crackdown-idUSBRE8630K120120704; "Oman Detains Poet, Blogger Amid Growing Discontent," Reuters, June 9, 2012,

http://uk.reuters.com/article/2012/06/09/oman-arrests-idUK
L5E8H91SB20120609; Human Rights Watch, *Oman: Assault on
Freedom of Speech*, June 13, 2012, http://www.hrw.org/news/2012/
06/13/oman-assault-freedom-speech.

20. Sa ̕id Sultan al-Hashimi (ed.), *al-rabi ̔ al-'Umani: qira'a fi al-
sayyaqat wa-l-dalalat* (The Omani Spring: A Reading of the Con-
texts and Meanings) (Beirut: Dar al-Farabi, 2013).

21. "Oman Ruler Pardons Jailed Dissidents," aljazeera.com,
March 23, 2013, http://www.aljazeera.com/news/middleeast/2013/
03/201332363737987137.html. One author argues that the notion of
fear that dominated Omani society and politics for decades had been
temporarily broken by the protests in early 2011. Khalid M. Al-Azri,
*Social and Gender Inequality in Oman: The Power of Religious and
Political Tradition* (Abingdon, UK: Routledge, 2013), xv-xviii, 141f.

22. Author's personal observations, Sohar, February 2013.

23. Christopher M. Davidson, "The United Arab Emirates:
Frontiers of the Arab Spring," *Open Democracy*, September 8, 2012,
www.opendemocracy.net/christopher-m-davidson/united-arab
-emirates-frontiers-of-arab-spring; Ingo Forstenlechner, Emilie Rut-
ledge, and Rashed Salem Alnuaimi, "The UAE, the 'Arab Spring'
and Different Types of Dissent," *Middle East Policy* 19, no. 4 (Winter 2012): 54–67.

24. http://www.ipetitions.com/petition/uaepetition71.

25. For details on the arrests, see Human Rights Watch reporting on the UAE, for example Human Rights Watch, *UAE: Trial
Observer Finds Due Process Flaws in "UAE 5" Case*, November 3,
2011, http://www.hrw.org/news/2011/11/03/uae-trial-observer-finds
-due-process-flaws-uae-5-case. See also Emirates Centre for Human
Rights, www.echr.org.uk. The forum, previously located at www
.uaehewar.net, was subsequently shut down. Christopher Davidson,
"The Strange Case of the UAE's WWW.UAEHEWAR.NET," *Current Intelligence*, November 15, 2010, http://www.currentintelli
gence.net/gulfstream/2010/11/15/the-strange-case-of-the-uaes
-wwwuaehewarnet.html.

26. The association's Arabic name is *jama'iyyat al-islah wa-l-tawjih al-ijtima'i*. Mansur al-Nuqaydan, "al-ikhwan al-muslimun fi al-Imarat: al-tamaddud wa-l-inhisar (The Muslim Brothers in the Emirates: Expansion and Decline)," in *al-ikhwan al-muslimun fi al-khalij (The Muslim Brotherhood in the Gulf)* (Dubai: Al Mesbar Studies and Research Centre, 2010), 55–105; "In the Gulf, Allegiance Is the Issue for Muslim Brotherhood," *The National*, January 30, 2012, http://www .thenational.ae/thenationalconversation/comment/in-the-gulf -allegiance-is-the-issue-for-muslim-brotherhood#page2; Ali Rashid al-Noaimi, "Setting the Record Straight on Al-Islah in the UAE," *Al-Monitor*, October 15, 2012, http://www.al-monitor.com/pulse/ originals/2012/al-monitor/uae-setting-the-record-straight.html. See the website of the group www.aleslaah.net and http://uaeseven-en .blogspot.co.uk. See also the al-Islah offshoot *hizb al-umma al-i marati* on Twitter @emiratesop. Some argue, however, that these political activists only retain very limited popularity in the UAE: Sultan Al Qassemi, "UAE Security Crackdown: A View from the Emirates," *Al-Monitor*, July 18, 2012, http://www.al-monitor.com/pulse/ originals/2012/al-monitor/the-uae-security-crackdown-a-vie.html.

27. "Rights Groups Urge Public Access to UAE Dissidents' Trial," Reuters, April 3, 2013, http://in.reuters.com/article/2013/04/03/ emirates-trial-rights-idINL5N0CQ22G20130403.

28. Kristian Coates Ulrichsen, "The UAE: Holding Back the Tide," *Open Democracy*, August 5, 2012, www.opendemocracy.net/ kristian-coates-ulrichsen/uae-holding-back-tide.

29. "Muslim Brotherhood Sows Subversion in Gulf—Dubai Police Chief," Reuters, April 3, 2013, http://uk.reuters.com/article/ 2013/04/03/uk-emirates-islamists-police-idUKBRE9320G8201 30403. For more on UAE-Egypt links and the crackdown in the UAE, see Christopher Davidson, *After the Sheikhs: The Coming Collapse of the Gulf Monarchies* (London: Hurst & Company, 2012), 202–204, 220–226.

30. Author interviews with Muslim Brotherhood activists, Kuwait, December 2012.

31. "Abou Hamed Flies to Dubai to Discuss New Party with Shafiq," *Al-Masry Al-Youm*, September 20, 2012, http://www.egyptindependent.com/news/abou-hamed-flies-dubai-discuss-new-party-shafiq.

32. Author interview with Bahraini economists, Manama, May 2011.

33. Thirty billion dirhams is approximately $8.2 billion. "Arab Spring Fund Flows to UAE Exceed $8 Billion: PM," Reuters, February 11, 2013, http://finance.yahoo.com/news/arab-spring-fund-flows-uae-130202750.html.

34. Due to high oil prices all the GCC states declared a budget surplus in 2011. "Robust Growth Projected for GCC," *Arab News*, June 24, 2012, http://www.arabnews.com/economy/robust-growth-projected-gcc.

35. In a similar vein, Qatar had for years mediated in a number of regional conflicts, including in Lebanon. Sultan Barakat, *The Qatari Spring: Qatar's Emerging Role in Peacemaking*, London School of Economics, Kuwait Research Programme, July 2012, http://www2.lse.ac.uk/government/research/resgroups/kuwait/research/papers/qatar.aspx.

36. Kristian Coates Ulrichsen, *Small States with a Big Role: Qatar and the United Arab Emirates in the Wake of the Arab Spring*, Durham University, 2012, http://www.dur.ac.uk/alsabah/publications/insights/no3ulrichsen, 12–18.

37. Ibid.

38. Guido Steinberg, "Qatar and the Arab Spring: Support for Islamists and New Anti-Syrian Policy," *SWP Comments 2012/C 07*, February 2012, http://www.swp-berlin.org/en/publications/swp-comments-en/swp-aktuelle-details/article/qatar_and_the_arab_spring.html; Hugh Eakin, "The Strange Power of Qatar," *The New York Review of Books*, October 27, 2011, http://www.nybooks.com/articles/archives/2011/oct/27/strange-power-qatar.

39. "There is no people's revolution in Bahrain but a sectarian one. . . . What is happening is not like what has happened in

Egypt, Tunisia and Libya, but it is the empowerment of some factions via foreign forces on others; thereby it does not include the demands of all of the Bahraini people." "Qaradawi Says Bahrain's Revolution Sectarian," *Al Arabiya News*, March 19, 2011, www .alarabiya.net/articles/2011/03/19/142205.html.

40. A group of Islamists allegedly petitioned the amir in 2011 to initiate reforms, but the petitions were not made public. Jane Kinninmont, "Qatar's Delicate Balancing Act," BBC, January 16, 2013, http://www.bbc.co.uk/news/world-middle-east-21029018.

41. Ali al-Kuwari, *al-sha'b yurid al-islah fi Qatar . . . aydan* (*The People Want Reform in Qatar . . . Too*) (Beirut: Muntada al-Ma'arif, 2012); Abdel Fattah Madi, "Qatari Activists Publish Blueprint for Reform," *Al-Monitor*, October 13, 2012, www.al-monitor.com/ pulse/politics/2012/10/how-to-call-for-reform-in-qatar.html.

42. Mohamed A. J. Althani, *The Arab Spring and the Gulf States: Time to Embrace Change* (London: Profile Books, 2012).

43. Author interviews with political analysts in UAE and Qatar, February 2013; Justin Gengler, "The Political Costs of Qatar's Western Orientation," *Middle East Policy* 19, no. 4 (Winter 2012): 68–76.

44. "Qatari Poet Jailed for Life After Writing Verse Inspired by Arab Spring," *The Guardian*, November 29, 2012, www.guardian .co.uk/world/2012/nov/29/qatari-poet-jailed-arab-spring.

45. "Qatar to Hold First National Election," *The Guardian*, November 1, 2011, http://www.guardian.co.uk/world/2011/nov/01/ qatar-to-hold-first-national-election.

46. For a recent overview, see Davidson, *After the Sheikhs*, 169–175.

47. Interview with a former Omani ambassador to Iran, Muscat, February 2013; Asghar Jafari-Valdani, "The Geopolitics of the Strait of Hormuz and the Iran-Oman Relations," *Iranian Review of Foreign Affairs* 2, no. 4 (Winter 2012): 7–40.

48. Steinberg, "Qatar and the Arab Spring," 5f.

49. Karim Sadjadpour, "The Battle of Dubai: The United Arab Emirates and the U.S.-Iran Cold War," Carnegie Endowment for

International Peace, July 27, 2011, http://carnegieendowment.org/2011/07/27/battle-of-dubai-united-arab-emirates-and-u.s.-iran-cold-war/8kiw.

50. "Oman Uncovers 'Spy Network' but UAE Denies Any Links," BBC, January 31, 2011, www.bbc.co.uk/news/world-middle-east-12320859; "How the Arab Spring Skirted Oman," *Huffington Post*, December 13, 2011, http://www.huffingtonpost.com/sigurd-neubauer/oman-arab-spring_b_1144473.html.

51. Marc Lynch, *The Arab Uprising: The Unfinished Revolutions of the New Middle East* (New York: PublicAffairs, 2012), 17f., 29–42.

52. Madawi al-Rasheed, "Saudi Arabia: Local and Regional Challenges," *Contemporary Arab Affairs* 6, no. 1 (2013): 28–40.

53. For background on the Saudi Muslim Brotherhood, see Stéphane Lacroix, *Awakening Islam: The Politics of Religious Dissent in Contemporary Saudi Arabia* (Cambridge, MA: Harvard University Press, 2011); Stéphane Lacroix, "Osama bin Laden and the Saudi Muslim Brotherhood," *Foreign Policy*, October 3, 2012, http://mideast.foreignpolicy.com/posts/2012/10/03/osama_bin_laden_and_the_saudi_muslim_brotherhood.

54. "Destination Riyadh," *al-Ahram Weekly*, July 12–18, 2012, http://weekly.ahram.org.eg/2012/1106/eg1.htm.

55. In April 2012, protesters gathered outside the Saudi embassy in Cairo, demanding the release of an Egyptian lawyer arrested in Saudi Arabia and denouncing the derogatory treatment of Egyptian visitors and expats in Saudi Arabia. As a result, the embassy was temporarily closed and the ambassador recalled, but he returned to Cairo a week later. "Egyptian Protests Over Detained Lawyer Shut Saudi Embassy," BBC, April 28, 2012, www.bbc.co.uk/news/world-middle-east-17881733.

56. "Misleading Translation or Height of Stupidity?" *Saudi Gazette*, September 03, 2012, www.saudigazette.com.sa/index.cfm?method=home.regcon&contentid=20120903134833.

57. "Islamische Kritik an der saudischen Regierung: Gespräch mit dem Kleriker Salman al-Audah," *Neue Zürcher Zeitung*, April 17, 2012, http://www.nzz.ch/aktuell/international/islamische-kritik

-an-der-saudischen-regierung-1.16481903. He later criticized, however, that the Saudi government was not doing enough in Syria,
and that it would not be possible to try to limit private Saudi
funding of the Syrian opposition and the exodus of Saudi youth
to fight in the Syrian war. "Citing U.S. Fears, Arab Allies Limit
Syrian Rebel Aid," *The New York Times*, October 7, 2012, http://
www.nytimes.com/2012/10/07/world/middleeast/citing-us
-fears-arab-allies-limit-aid-to-syrian-rebels.html.

58. This is most strikingly recounted by a young Alawite
woman who became an anti-regime activist in the Syrian revolution: Samar Yazbek, *A Woman in the Crossfire: Diaries of the Syrian
Revolution*, trans. Max Weiss (London: Haus, 2012).

59. Saudi Arabia and Qatar have said that they provide military
assistance to the rebels in Syria. "Citing U.S. Fears, Arab Allies
Limit Syrian Rebel Aid."

60. Justin Gengler, "Bahraini Salafis Fighting the Infidels
Wherever They Find Them," August 6, 2012, http://bahrainipolitics
.blogspot.co.uk/2012/08/bahraini-salafis-fighting-infidels.html. See
also "al-Manama: jadal ba'd ziyyara nuwwab bahrayniyyin li-Suriya
(Manama: Dispute After a Visit of Bahraini MPs to Syria)," *CNN
Arabic*, August 6, 2012, http://arabic.cnn.com/2012/middle_
east/8/6/Bahraini-BMs-Syria/index.html.

61. "'Dozens of Kuwaiti Jihadists' Join Different Nationalities
to Enlist in Free Syrian Army," *Al Arabiya News*, June 10, 2012,
http://english.alarabiya.net/articles/2012/06/10/219734.html;
"Saudi Steers Citizens Away from Syrian 'Jihad'," Reuters, September 12, 2012, http://www.reuters.com/article/2012/09/12/us
-saudi-syria-jihad-idUSBRE88B0XY20120912.

62. "Saudi-Based Syrian Cleric Urges Continued Protests
Against Assad's Regime," *Al Arabiya News*, August 6, 2011, http://
www.alarabiya.net/articles/2011/08/06/161116.html; "Sheikh
Adnan Arour's Meteoric Rise from Obscurity to Notoriety," *The
National*, July 5, 2012, http://www.thenational.ae/news/world/
middle-east/sheikh-adnan-arours-meteoric-rise-from-obscurity-
to-notoriety. He returned to Syria in September 2012 and appeared

at a press conference of the Revolutionary Military Councils. There are debates about whether sectarianism is indeed such a key part of his ideology. Joshua Landis, "Sheikh Arour Becomes Icon of the Revolutionary Military Councils," *Syria Comment*, October 7, 2012, http://www.joshualandis.com/blog/?p=16341&cp=all. With over one million followers on Twitter as of April 14, 2013, @AdnanAlarour is possibly the Syrian with the most followers on the social media network.

63. A Syrian activist critical of the sectarian rhetoric argues, "Religion is a major rallying force in this revolution—look at Ara'our [a sectarian preacher], he is hysterical and we don't like him but he offers unquestionable support to the fighters and they need it." "Al-Qaida Turns Tide for Rebels in Battle for Eastern Syria," *The Guardian*, July 30, 2012, http://www.guardian.co.uk/world/2012/jul/30/al-qaida-rebels-battle-syria.

64. Laurence Louër, *Transnational Shiite Politics: Religious and Political Networks in the Gulf* (New York: Columbia University Press, 2008), 196–198; Sabrina Mervin, "Sayyida Zaynab, Banlieue de Damas ou nouvelle ville sainte chiite?" *Cahiers d'Études sur la Méditerranée Orientale et le Monde Turco-Iranien* 22 (1996): 149–162; Khalid Sindawi, "The Shiite Turn in Syria," *Current Trends in Islamist Ideology* 8 (June 23, 2009): 82–107; Edith Szanto, "Sayyida Zaynab in the State of Exception: Shi'i Sainthood as 'Qualified Life' in Contemporary Syria," *International Journal of Middle East Studies* 44 (2012): 285–299.

65. In early August 2012, forty-eight Iranians were captured by the Free Syrian Army in Damascus, at least the third such incident since the start of the protests in Syria. Iran argued that the Iranians were pilgrims traveling to Sayyida Zeinab. They were released in January 2013. "Three of the Iranians Abducted in Syria killed," *The Daily News Egypt*, August 7, 2012, http://thedailynewsegypt.com/2012/08/07/three-of-the-iranians-abducted-in-syria-killed; "Iranian Captives Freed in Prisoner Exchange in Syria," *The New York Times*, January 9, 2013, http://www.nytimes.com/2013/01/10/world/middleeast/syria-iranians-prisoner-exchange.html.

66. Author interview with Lebanese political analyst, Beirut, March 2013; "Video Appears to Show Hezbollah and Iraqi Shiites Fighting in Syria," *The Christian Science Monitor*, January 18, 2013, http://www.csmonitor.com/World/Middle-East/2013/0118/Video -appears-to-show-Hezbollah-and-Iraqi-Shiites-fighting-in-Syria.

67. "As Syrian War Drags On, Jihadists Take Bigger Role," *The New York Times*, July 29, 2012, http://www.nytimes.com/2012/07/30/ world/middleeast/as-syrian-war-drags-on-jihad-gains-foothold.html. For a detailed analysis of the *salafi* and *jihadi* groups in the Syrian opposition, see International Crisis Group, *Tentative Jihad: Syria's Fundamentalist Opposition*, October 12, 2012, http://www.crisis group.org/en/regions/middle-east-north-africa/egypt-syria-lebanon/ syria/131-tentative-jihad-syrias-fundamentalist-opposition.aspx.

68. Lebanese Hizbullah's support for the Assad regime during the Syrian uprising eroded the support it had amongst many Sunnis in the region. For more, see International Crisis Group, *Syria's Mutating Conflict*, August 1, 2012, 30, http://www.crisisgroup.org/ en/regions/middle-east-north-africa/egypt-syria-lebanon/syria/ 128-syrias-mutating-conflict.aspx

69. For accounts of the fighting by Shia living in Sayyida Zeinab, see "The Whole Story of What Happened in Sayyidah Zainab Area, Syria," RNI News Agency, August 3, 2012, http://www.realnewslive .org/eng/2012/08/03/the-whole-story-of-what-happened-in -sayyidah-zainab-area-syria; and "The Current Situation in Sayyidah Zainab Area 24/7/2012," Shii News Email Newsletter, http://www .husainiyouths.org/profiles/blogs/the-current-situation-in-sayyidah -zainab-area-syria-24-7-2012.

70. Hassan Hassan, "Why Tribes Matter in Syria," *The Guardian*, July 25, 2012, http://www.guardian.co.uk/commentisfree/2012/ jul/25/syria-tribal-rivalries-shape-future; "Saudi Support for Syrian Rebels Shaped by Tribal, Religious Ties," CNN, August 20, 2012, http://edition.cnn.com/2012/08/20/world/meast/syria-saudi-aid.

71. Much of this was directed against Qatar. "Assad Intensifies Cyberwar Against Qatar," *Financial Times*, April 24, 2012, http:// www.ft.com/cms/s/0/1fa5d708-8e1c-11e1-bf8f-00144feab49a.html;

Michael Stephens, "Syria: Silent War in the Gulf," *Open Democracy*, August 19, 2012, www.opendemocracy.net/michael-stephens/syria-silent-war-in-gulf.

72. See, for example, "In Bahrain, Worries Grow of Violent Shiite-Sunni Confrontation," *The New York Times*, January 25, 2012, http://www.nytimes.com/2012/01/26/world/middleeast/26iht-m26-bahrain-conflict.html.

73. Muqtada al-Sadr called for demonstrations in solidarity with Bahrain and issued a statement calling for the boycott of the 2012 F1 race in Bahrain. "Sayyid Muqtada al-Sadr Answers Question on Formula Race in Bahrain," *al-Sadr Online*, April 18, 2012, http://www.alsadronline.net/en/news/4247-sayyid-muqtada-al-sadr-answers-question-on-bahraini-prisoners.html. "Sadrists Rally in Basra to Support Bahraini People," *Aswat al-Iraq*, March 19, 2012, http://en.aswataliraq.info/%28S%28k4khqp55exzt5urwzn fxh045%29%29/printer.aspx?id=147514.

74. "Grand Ayatollah Sistani Condemns the Saudi and Bahrain's Force Crackdown on Bahrain's Shia, While Kuwait Refuses to Send Troops," *Jafria News*, March 17, 2011, http://jafrianews.com/2011/03/17/grand-ayatollah-sistani-condemns-the-saudi-and-bahrains-force-crackdown-on-bahrains-shia-while-kuwait-refuses-to-send-troops; "Shiites Rally Behind Bahrain Protesters," Agence France-Presse, Mar 17, 2011, www.abc.net.au/news/2011-03-17/shiites-rally-behind-bahrain-protesters/2653372.

75. Ghanim Jawad, an Iraqi Shia political analyst, interview with author, London, September 2011.

76. Toby Dodge, *Iraq: From War to a New Authoritarianism* (London: International Institute for Strategic Studies and Routledge, 2012).

77. "Sunni Protests in Iraq," *al-Ahram Weekly*, April 5–11, 2012, http://weekly.ahram.org.eg/2012/1092/re1.htm; International Crisis Group, *Déjà Vu All Over Again: Iraq's Escalating Political Crisis*, July 30, 2012, http://www.crisisgroup.org/en/regions/middle-east-north-africa/iraq-iran-gulf/iraq/126-deja-vu-all-over-again-iraqs-escalating-political-crisis.aspx; International Crisis Group, *Iraq's*

Secular Opposition: The Rise and Decline of Al-Iraqiya, July 31, 2012, http://www.crisisgroup.org/en/regions/middle-east-north-africa/iraq-iran-gulf/iraq/127-iraqs-secular-opposition-the-rise-and-decline-of-al-iraqiya.aspx. Al-Hashimi initially fled from Baghdad to the semi-autonomous Kurdish region in Northern Iraq, then on to Qatar, and finally to Turkey. In September 2012, al-Hashimi—before his indictment the most senior Sunni politician in Iraq—was sentenced to death in absentia in Iraq. "Iraq VP Tariq al-Hashemi Sentenced to Death," BBC, September 9, 2012, http://www.bbc.co.uk/news/world-middle-east-19537301.

78. The army shot several protesters in Anbar province in January 2013. "Iraq Sunnis Threaten Army Attacks After Protest Deaths," BBC, January 26, 2013, http://www.bbc.co.uk/news/world-middle-east-21206163.

79. "Sunni spring" is a hashtag used on Twitter in Arabic. Fanar Haddad, "Can a Sunni Spring Turn into an Iraqi Spring?" *Foreign Policy*, January 7, 2013, http://mideast.foreignpolicy.com/posts/2013/01/07/can_a_sunni_spring_turn_into_an_iraqi_spring.

80. "Sleiman to UAE to Discuss Reported Expulsion of Lebanese," *The Daily Star*, June 6, 2012, http://www.dailystar.com.lb/News/Politics/2012/Jun-06/175891-sleiman-to-uae-to-discuss-reported-expulsion-of-lebanese.ashx.

81. "Bahrain Expels 16 Lebanese Amid Unrest," Agence France-Presse, April 11, 2011, http://al-shorfa.com/en_GB/articles/meii/features/main/2011/04/13/feature-02.

82. "Aoun: Bahrain Remarks Not Interference, Just Advice," *Daily Star*, February 19, 2013, http://www.dailystar.com.lb/News/Politics/2013/Feb-19/207108-aoun-bahrain-remarks-not-interference-just-advice.ashx#axzz2PrueQDbn.

CONCLUSION

1. "Thousands of Shia Muslims Protest Over Gulf Union Plans," BBC, May 18, 2012, http://www.bbc.co.uk/news/world-middle-east-18120787; Frederic Wehrey, "The March of Bahrain's Hardliners,"

Carnegie Middle East Center, May 2012, http://carnegie-mec.org/publications/?fa=48299.

2. The Omani foreign minister, Yousuf bin Alawi, has publicly said that Oman does not want the union and that it will not be realized. "Ibn 'Alawi: fikrat al-ittihad la yastawa'bha al-jil al-hali" (Ibn 'Alawi: The Current Generation Does Not Fully Understand the Idea of 'Union'), *'Uman*, March 21, 2012, http://main.omandaily.om/node/88945; "Oman's Foreign Minister Says There Is No Gulf Union," *Gulf News*, June 6, 2012, http://gulfnews.com/news/gulf/oman/oman-s-foreign-minister-says-there-is-no-gulf-union-1.1032092.

3. Author interviews with officials and intellectuals in the UAE, Qatar, Oman, and Kuwait, February–March 2013.

4. "GCC Ministers Sign Security Pact," *Arab News*, November 14, 2012, www.arabnews.com/gcc-ministers-sign-security-pact.

5. "Bahrain Blames Iran for 'Terror Cell'," *Gulf News*, February, 20, 2013, http://gulfnews.com/news/gulf/bahrain/bahrain-blames-iran-for-terror-cell-1.1148578.

6. Christopher Davidson, *After the Sheikhs: The Coming Collapse of the Gulf Monarchies* (London: Hurst & Company, 2012).

7. These figureheads include people such as Abd al-Hadi al-Khawaja or Hasan Mushayma in Bahrain, Nimr al-Nimr or Muhammad al-Qahtani in Saudi Arabia, and Musallam al-Barrak in Kuwait. At the time of writing (April 2013), all these opposition leaders are either in jail or on trial.

8. For the original idea of the rentier state, see Hazem Beblawi, "The Rentier State in the Arab World," in *The Rentier State*, ed. Giacomo Luciani and Hazem Beblawi, 49–62 (London: Croom Helm, 1987).

9. Kristian Coates Ulrichsen, *Insecure Gulf: The End of Certainty and the Transition to the Post-Oil Era* (London: Hurst & Company, 2011).

10. In March 2011, the GCC pledged to support its poorest members, Bahrain and Oman, each with a $10 billion aid package over ten years to allow the governments to invest in infrastructure

and higher salaries in order to buy off opposition through hand-outs of wealth. "GCC to Set Up $20bn Bailout Fund for Bahrain and Oman," *The National*, March 11, 2011, http://www.thenational.ae/news/world/middle-east/gcc-to-set-up-20bn-bailout-fund-for-bahrain-and-oman.

11. Glada Lahn and Paul Stevens, *Burning Oil to Keep Cool: The Hidden Energy Crisis in Saudi Arabia*, Chatham House programme report, December 2011, http://www.chathamhouse.org/publications/papers/view/180825; "Saudi Arabia May Become Net Oil Importer By 2030: Citigroup," *Economy Watch*, September 5, 2012, http://www.economywatch.com/in-the-news/saudi-arabia-may-become-net-oil-importer-by-2030.05-09.html.

GLOSSARY

A note on transliteration: For the sake of readability, Arabic transliteration in this book was confined to some key terms, and to Arabic sources cited in the endnotes. Arabic names of people, places, and organizations are spelled in the way they are most commonly used in English.

ʿAJAM lit. non-Arab; in Iraq and the Gulf it has come to denote Shia of Iranian descent

AL the house of or the clan of

AMIR governor, ruler (in Kuwait and Qatar)

ASHURA tenth day of the month of *Muharram*; commemoration of the martyrdom of Hussayn, the Prophet Muhammad's grandson and third imam in Shia Islam, in 680

AYATOLLAH lit. sign of God; title for a senior *mujtahid*

BAHRANI, PL. BAHARNA self-description of the long-standing inhabitants of Bahrain, and the term used in British colonial records; the *Baharna* are largely Shia

BIDUN lit. *bidun jinsiyya*, without citizenship; name for stateless people in the Gulf

DIWAN Salon, reception area in a house, or a separate building, where *diwaniyyas* are held, called *majlis* in some countries such as Saudi Arabia and Qatar

DIWANIYYA salon evening; a semi-private discussion forum or gathering, particularly popular in Kuwait

HASAWI originally from al-Ahsa

HUSSAINIYYA Shia mourning house for the commemoration of the martyrdom of Hussayn, also community centers; in some countries hussainiyyas are also referred to as *ma'tam*

IBADI, IBADIYYA sect of Islam; a majority of Omani citizens are *Ibadis*

IMAM one of the twelve recognized hereditary successors of the Prophet Muhammad in Twelver Shia Islam

JIHAD lit. struggle; here used in the sense of holy war against infidels to expand the territory of Islam

KHALIJI Gulf Arab citizen, deriving from the Arabic name for the Gulf, *al-Khalij*

LAWATI, LAWATIYYA group of Shia in Oman that largely migrated from India between the mid-eighteenth century and the end of the nineteenth century

LEFTIST here used as a term describing all varieties of secular, nationalist, and left-wing groups active in the Gulf

MAJLIS seating area in a house; salon or reception room; referred to as *Diwan* in some countries

MAJLIS AL-SHURA Consultative Council

MARJI' AL-TAQLID lit. reference point for emulation; someone who is qualified through his learning and probity to be followed in all points of religious practice and law by the generality of Shia muslims

MARJI'IYYA authority, the institution of *marji' al-taqlid*

MA'TAM Shia mourning house, name often used in Bahrain, like a *hussainiyya*

MUDARRISIYYA a group that split away from the *shiraziyya*, made up of people who decided to follow the *marji'iyya* of Muhammad Taqi al-Mudarrisi and his brother Hadi al-Mudarrisi after the death of Muhammad Mahdi al-Shirazi (1928–2001); the mudarrisiyya continued a confrontational approach toward the Gulf governments, including during the Arab Spring

MUJTAHID a cleric who has reached the level of competence and scholarship necessary to perform *ijtihad*, independent legal judgment in matters of religious law

SALAFI, SALAFIYYA those who wish to follow the example of the first generation of Muslims, the *al-salaf al-salih* (pious ancestors)

SHABAB young men

SHAYKHI, SHAYKHIYYA followers of Ahmad al-Ahsa'i (1753–1826), esoteric strand of Shia Islam; retains some following in Saudi Arabia, Kuwait, Iran, and Iraq; sometimes deemed heretical by other Twelver Shia scholars

SHIRAZI, SHIRAZIYYA transnational Shia political network, whose name derives from its deceased spiritual leader, Muhammad Mahdi al-Shirazi (1928–2001)

UMMA community of Muslim believers

WAHHABI, WAHHABIYYA followers of Muhammad ibn 'Abd al-Wahhab (1703–1792), whose teachings centered on the oneness of God (*tawhid*) and who wanted to purify Islam from innovations

INDEX

Page numbers in italic type indicate photographs.

Made in the USA
Middletown, DE
06 January 2018